The VR Developer's Guide

Creating Immersive Experiences with Unreal Engine Build virtual worlds and immersive experiences with game engines

THOMPSON CARTER

All rights reserved

Table of Content

TABLE OF CONTENTS

INTRODUCTION

The VR Developer's Guide: Creating Immersive Experiences with Unreal Engine

In recent years, Virtual Reality (VR) has emerged as one of the most exciting and transformative technologies across various industries. From gaming and entertainment to education, healthcare, and real estate, VR has revolutionized how we experience digital environments. However, despite its explosive growth, the process of creating compelling and immersive VR experiences is still in its infancy, with numerous challenges and opportunities for developers to explore.

This book, **"The VR Developer's Guide: Creating Immersive Experiences with Unreal Engine"**, serves as a comprehensive guide to understanding and mastering the art of VR development. It is tailored for both beginners looking to dive into the world of VR and experts seeking to enhance their existing knowledge. Whether you are looking to create VR games, simulations, or applications for any industry, this guide will provide you with the tools, techniques, and best practices to create truly immersive and interactive VR environments.

Why This Book?

In the past decade, Unreal Engine has firmly established itself as one of the leading platforms for VR development. With its powerful visual capabilities, user-friendly interfaces, and flexibility, Unreal Engine offers developers the perfect environment to bring their VR ideas to life. By combining both **Blueprints**, a visual scripting tool, and **C++**, a more advanced programming language, Unreal Engine allows developers to create detailed, high-performance VR applications with a variety of interaction models, from simple games to complex, interactive simulations.

But while Unreal Engine's capabilities are vast, VR development comes with its unique set of challenges. Performance optimization, creating intuitive interactions, handling motion sickness, and ensuring high frame rates are just a few of the hurdles VR developers must overcome. Additionally, VR development requires a deep understanding of both the hardware and software aspects—how VR headsets, controllers, and sensors work, as well as how to leverage the power of Unreal Engine to create responsive and engaging content.

This book was written with these challenges in mind. It equips you with the essential skills, practical knowledge, and real-world examples necessary to successfully develop VR applications using Unreal Engine. Whether you are a game developer aiming to create the next immersive VR experience, a professional looking to implement VR solutions in healthcare or education, or simply someone fascinated by the potential of virtual environments, this book will guide you through the entire VR development process.

What Will You Learn?

Throughout the chapters of this book, you will learn the foundational concepts of VR development, such as how VR works and how to build immersive worlds from scratch. By starting with a deep dive into **Unreal Engine**, you'll be equipped with the tools you need to create dynamic VR environments, from **interactive physics** to **real-time**

rendering and **custom input systems**. You'll also gain insights into the hardware that powers VR experiences, ensuring that you understand the strengths and limitations of different VR platforms and can optimize your projects accordingly.

The book covers a range of important topics, including:

1. **Core VR Development Concepts**: How to build and optimize VR environments for high immersion and interaction.

2. **Unreal Engine Mastery**: Learn both Blueprint scripting and C++ programming, as well as how to use Unreal Engine's tools to build VR worlds.

3. **Interaction and Movement**: Create seamless movement systems, from teleportation to smooth locomotion, and advanced interaction systems using hand tracking and controllers.

4. **Performance Optimization**: Learn to tackle common performance issues in VR and ensure smooth, high-performance experiences.

5. **VR Audio and Cinematics**: How to design spatial audio systems and cinematic experiences to enhance immersion.

6. **Testing and Debugging**: Understand how to effectively test and debug your VR applications to ensure they are comfortable and bug-free.

7. **The Future of VR**: Explore the upcoming trends in VR and how to future-proof your projects, from AI integration to cloud-based VR and mixed reality.

By the end of the book, you will have the skills to design, develop, and deploy your own VR applications, whether you're creating **games**, **training simulations**, or **virtual tours**. You'll also be prepared to tackle common pitfalls and keep your projects up to date with the latest VR advancements.

Why Unreal Engine?

You might be wondering: Why focus specifically on **Unreal Engine** for VR development? Unreal Engine is widely regarded as one of the most powerful and flexible game engines on the market, and it excels in VR development for several key reasons:

- **High-Quality Graphics**: Unreal Engine is renowned for its ability to produce cutting-edge graphics, which is essential for creating immersive VR environments. The engine's **real-time rendering** capabilities allow developers to produce stunning visuals that are critical for VR experiences.

- **Blueprints and C++**: Unreal's combination of **Blueprints** (a visual scripting language) and **C++** (a more traditional coding language) offers versatility, making it accessible to beginners while still offering depth for experienced developers.

- **VR-Optimized Tools**: Unreal Engine provides a dedicated **VR Template** that helps developers get started quickly, and it offers built-in support for a wide range of VR hardware, including **Oculus Rift, HTC Vive, PlayStation VR**, and others. The engine also provides easy integration for **hand tracking, eye tracking**, and **motion controllers**.

- **Large Community and Resources**: Unreal Engine has a huge developer community, rich documentation, and numerous tutorials available, making it easier for you to find solutions to common problems and learn from other developers.

Who Should Read This Book?

11

This book is designed for anyone interested in developing VR applications, whether you are a **beginner**, an **experienced game developer**, or someone working in fields like **education, healthcare, architecture**, or **training simulation**. If you have an interest in VR, and especially if you're already familiar with Unreal Engine, this book will deepen your understanding and provide you with practical knowledge that you can immediately apply to your projects.

- **Beginner Developers**: If you're just starting out with VR development or Unreal Engine, this book provides the perfect introduction, starting with the basics and gradually advancing into more complex topics.

- **Experienced Developers**: If you're already an Unreal Engine user, this book will help you transition from traditional game development to VR, teaching you advanced techniques for creating immersive environments and solving VR-specific challenges.

- **Non-Game Developers**: VR is also used in many industries outside gaming, such as **healthcare, education, architecture**, and **training**. This book will show you how to create VR simulations that can be used in a wide range of applications beyond gaming.

The Journey Ahead

The potential of VR is limitless, and by mastering the tools and techniques covered in this book, you will be ready to join the ranks of VR developers who are pushing the boundaries of what's possible in digital experiences. Whether you're crafting the next big VR game, building educational simulations, or designing immersive training programs, this guide will give you the foundation and expertise to create truly immersive and interactive virtual worlds.

Let's dive in and explore the exciting world of VR development!

CHAPTER 1

INTRODUCTION TO VR DEVELOPMENT

Overview of Virtual Reality (VR)

Definition of Virtual Reality (VR): Virtual Reality (VR) refers to the use of computer-generated environments that simulate real-world or imagined experiences. By using specialized equipment like VR headsets and controllers, users can immerse themselves in these digital worlds, allowing them to interact with and experience the environment in a way that feels lifelike.

Evolution of VR:

- **1960s - The Beginnings**: The concept of VR dates back to the 1960s, when computer scientist Ivan Sutherland developed the first rudimentary head-mounted display system. This early version of VR was known as "The Sword of Damocles" and was more of a research project than a consumer product.

- **1990s - The Early Commercial Attempts**: In the 1990s, VR technology started to make its way into the consumer

14

market. Companies like Sega and Nintendo attempted to introduce VR gaming systems, but limitations in computing power and high costs made these products less than successful.

- **2010s - VR's Revival**: The arrival of Oculus Rift (acquired by Facebook) in 2012, along with HTC Vive and PlayStation VR, marked a significant turning point. These devices provided much more refined and accessible VR experiences, making VR a reality for gamers, developers, and businesses alike.

- **Present Day & Future**: Today, VR technology is at the forefront of immersive entertainment, healthcare, education, and even business. With companies like Oculus (Meta), HTC, and Sony constantly improving hardware, VR is becoming more affordable, lightweight, and user-friendly. The future of VR is not just about entertainment; it's expanding into fields like medicine (for therapy), education (for interactive learning), and remote work (virtual collaboration spaces).

Future Prospects of VR: The VR industry is projected to continue growing, with advancements in hardware and software making VR more realistic, interactive, and accessible. Key areas to watch include:

- **Full-Body Motion Capture**: More precise body tracking technologies will enhance immersion.

- **Mixed Reality (MR)**: Combining AR and VR to allow for more seamless interaction with the physical and digital worlds.
- **AI and Machine Learning**: Enhancing interactivity by making virtual characters smarter and more responsive.

Why Unreal Engine for VR

Unreal Engine (UE) is one of the most widely-used game engines in the world, and it has proven itself to be a powerful tool for VR development. Here's why Unreal Engine is the engine of choice for VR developers:

1. **Visual Fidelity**: Unreal Engine is renowned for its stunning graphical output. It can handle complex shaders, lighting, and textures with a level of detail that enhances immersion. In VR, where realism is crucial for the sense of presence, Unreal's capabilities allow developers to create visually compelling worlds.

2. **Blueprints Visual Scripting**: Unreal Engine's Blueprints system allows developers to create complex gameplay mechanics and interactions without writing a single line of code. This is particularly beneficial for beginners who may not have programming experience but still want to build powerful VR experiences.

16

3. **Native VR Support**: Unreal Engine comes with built-in support for VR development, including integration with headsets like Oculus Rift, HTC Vive, and PlayStation VR. It has optimized tools for motion controllers, interaction systems, and spatial audio, making it a perfect choice for VR developers.

4. **Cross-Platform Development**: With Unreal Engine, developers can create VR experiences that can be easily deployed across multiple platforms. Whether it's PC VR, standalone VR like Oculus Quest, or even console-based VR like PSVR, Unreal's tools make cross-platform VR development seamless.

5. **Real-Time Rendering**: Unreal Engine excels at real-time rendering, which is essential for VR development where frame rates and latency are critical to user comfort. High-quality real-time rendering ensures that VR experiences are smooth and immersive, with minimal delay.

6. **Community and Resources**: Unreal Engine has a large and active community of developers, which means there are plenty of tutorials, forums, and resources to help you get started and troubleshoot any issues you encounter. Additionally, Epic Games, the creators of Unreal Engine, offer a range of free assets and plugins to speed up development.

Basic VR Terminology

To help navigate the world of VR development, it's essential to understand some basic VR terminology:

1. **Immersion**:

   Immersion refers to the feeling of being fully engrossed in a virtual environment. The more immersive a VR experience is, the more a user feels like they are truly present in the virtual world. Immersion is achieved through a combination of high-quality visuals, 3D spatial audio, responsive interaction, and motion tracking.

2. **Interaction**:

   Interaction refers to the ways in which users engage with the virtual world. In VR, interaction can take many forms: from grabbing objects and pressing buttons to navigating the environment or communicating with virtual characters. Interaction is what makes VR experiences feel real and dynamic. For VR development, it's critical to design interactions that are intuitive and responsive.

3. **Presence**:

   Presence is the psychological state in which users feel like they are physically located in a virtual environment. It's the highest level of immersion. Achieving presence in VR requires consistent and seamless interaction, a high-quality environment, and natural user feedback, such as realistic hand movements, environmental sounds, and physical sensations.

4. **Head Tracking**: Head tracking is the process by which a VR system monitors and responds to the movement of the user's head. This allows the virtual environment to adjust accordingly, ensuring that the user sees the correct perspective as they look around. This is essential for creating the feeling of being inside the VR world.

5. **FOV (Field of View)**: FOV refers to the extent of the observable environment at any given moment. In VR, FOV is critical for immersion. A narrow FOV can make the virtual world feel claustrophobic, while a wide FOV increases the sensation of presence and openness.

Real-World Example: VR Applications in Gaming, Healthcare, and Education

1. **Gaming**: VR has revolutionized the gaming industry by creating truly immersive experiences. Games like *Half-Life: Alyx*, *Beat Saber*, and *Superhot VR* offer players the opportunity to engage with game worlds in ways traditional gaming cannot. Whether it's wielding a lightsaber or solving puzzles in a first-person

environment, VR gaming has redefined interactive entertainment.

2. **Healthcare**:

   VR is being used in healthcare for both treatment and training. In therapy, VR can help patients overcome phobias, anxiety, and PTSD by immersing them in controlled, therapeutic environments. For example, *Bravemind*, a VR-based PTSD treatment program, helps veterans re-live and process traumatic experiences in a safe and controlled manner. VR is also used for medical training, allowing doctors to practice surgeries and medical procedures without any risk.

3. **Education**:

   VR is transforming education by offering interactive learning experiences. For instance, VR in schools can provide students with virtual field trips, allowing them to "visit" historical landmarks, space stations, or even the human body. Programs like *Google Expeditions* are already helping students to learn in a highly engaging and immersive way, opening doors to new ways of education beyond textbooks.

This chapter sets the stage for a deeper dive into VR development, making it clear why VR is important, how Unreal Engine supports its creation, and how foundational concepts like immersion, interaction, and presence are key to crafting truly immersive experiences. Each section builds toward the understanding that VR development is not just about technology but also about enhancing user experience across industries.

CHAPTER 2

UNDERSTANDING GAME ENGINES AND UNREAL ENGINE

What is a Game Engine?

Basics of Game Engines: A **game engine** is a software framework designed for the development of video games. It provides developers with the essential tools needed to build and manage the various elements of a game, such as graphics, physics, sound, and input handling. Game engines are responsible for bringing a game to life by offering features that handle:

- **Rendering**: Drawing the visual elements (e.g., characters, environments).
- **Physics**: Simulating realistic movement, collisions, and interactions.
- **Sound**: Integrating music, sound effects, and voice acting.
- **Animation**: Making characters and objects move and react to events.
- **Artificial Intelligence (AI)**: Creating intelligent behaviors for in-game entities.

- **Networking**: Enabling multiplayer and communication features.

For VR development, game engines take on an even greater role. VR applications require a higher degree of realism, interactivity, and optimization. A game engine's role is crucial in delivering smooth, immersive experiences that minimize latency and motion sickness, which are essential for VR applications.

Role in VR Development: In the context of VR, a game engine does much more than just rendering graphics and handling inputs. It coordinates the complex interactions between user movements, environmental changes, and interactive elements in real-time. Game engines like Unreal Engine allow VR developers to:

- **Create immersive, interactive environments**.
- **Handle real-time 3D rendering and motion tracking**.
- **Integrate spatial audio for more realistic sound**.
- **Provide support for VR hardware like motion controllers and headsets**.
- **Ensure smooth performance, maintaining a high frame rate for comfort**.

The Unreal Engine Advantage

Unreal Engine (UE) has become one of the most popular and powerful game engines used for VR development. Here's why Unreal Engine is a top choice for VR developers:

1. **High-Quality Graphics and Visual Fidelity**: Unreal Engine is known for its stunning graphical capabilities, making it the engine of choice for developers aiming for photorealistic environments. For VR, this is critical. A high level of detail helps create a more immersive experience where users feel truly "inside" the world. With Unreal's real-time rendering features, developers can produce beautiful, dynamic scenes that react to user interactions.

2. **Blueprints Visual Scripting**: Unreal Engine's **Blueprints** system is one of the most significant advantages for VR developers, especially for those who may not have strong coding skills. Blueprints provide a visual way to script gameplay elements without the need to write C++ code. This system is powerful enough for complex VR interactions, such as object manipulation, player movement, and environmental responses, while still being beginner-friendly.

3. **Native VR Support**: Unreal Engine offers built-in support for VR headsets like Oculus Rift, HTC Vive, and PlayStation VR. The engine

includes specific VR templates that developers can use to jump-start their VR projects. This means that the heavy lifting of setting up interactions, rendering, and performance optimization is already handled, saving developers time and effort.

4. **Cross-Platform Development**: Unreal Engine makes it easier to deploy VR applications across multiple platforms. Whether it's PC VR, console-based VR, or standalone headsets like the Oculus Quest, Unreal's support for cross-platform VR development ensures that developers can target a broader audience with minimal extra effort.

5. **Real-Time Rendering and Performance Optimization**: In VR, smooth performance is crucial to maintaining immersion and preventing discomfort. Unreal Engine excels at real-time rendering, meaning it can generate high-quality visuals without significant performance hits. It also comes with built-in tools to optimize frame rates and reduce latency, ensuring that VR applications run smoothly.

6. **Robust Community and Resources**: Unreal Engine has a vast and active community of developers, designers, and artists. This community regularly shares tutorials, forums, and troubleshooting tips, making it easier for both beginners and professionals to learn and solve problems. Epic Games, the creator of

Unreal Engine, provides extensive documentation, free assets, and plugins to aid in VR development.

Setting Up Unreal Engine for VR Development

Getting started with Unreal Engine for VR development requires a few key steps. Let's go through the process:

1. **Download and Install Unreal Engine**:
   - **Visit the Unreal Engine website**: Go to Unreal Engine's official site and create an account if you don't already have one.
   - **Download the Epic Games Launcher**: The launcher is the tool you use to access Unreal Engine. Once installed, open the launcher, and you can download the latest version of Unreal Engine.
   - **Choose the Right Version**: Make sure you are using the version of Unreal Engine that supports VR development. Unreal 4.x or the latest Unreal 5.x versions both provide full VR support.
2. **Install VR Plugins and Set Up the Project**:
   - Once Unreal Engine is installed, open the **Epic Games Launcher** and launch Unreal Engine.
   - **Create a New Project**: From the Unreal Engine interface, select "Games" under the new project

options, and choose a **VR Template**. This template is specifically designed to help you start with VR interactions, movement, and basic setup.

o **Add VR Plugins**: If you are developing for specific VR hardware (e.g., Oculus, Vive, or PlayStation VR), you may need to enable certain plugins within Unreal Engine. This can be done from the **Plugins** menu, where you can activate support for VR devices like motion controllers and headsets.

3. **Configuring the VR Settings**:

o In the project settings, make sure the **VR Mode** is enabled. This will activate various VR-specific features in the engine, including head-tracking, motion controller integration, and support for 3D spatial audio.

o **Optimize Settings**: VR requires a higher frame rate than traditional games to maintain immersion. Go to the **Engine Scalability Settings** and adjust them to ensure smooth performance, aiming for 90 FPS or higher if possible.

o **Connect Your VR Hardware**: Plug in your VR headset (e.g., Oculus Rift or HTC Vive) and ensure it's recognized by Unreal Engine. Check the VR settings in the editor to confirm that the headset and controllers are working.

4. **Test Your Setup**:

   o Before diving into development, it's always a good idea to test your setup. Load up the default VR template project and put on your headset. You should see the environment rendered in 3D, and you should be able to move your head around and interact with simple objects.

   o **Tweak settings** for comfort, such as the comfort zone (for reducing motion sickness) and controller sensitivity, until everything feels right.

Real-World Example: "Beat Saber" — A VR Game Developed with Unreal Engine

Overview:

One of the most successful VR games that has showcased the power of Unreal Engine is *Beat Saber*. Developed by Beat Games, *Beat Saber* is a rhythm-based game where players use VR motion controllers to slice through blocks representing musical beats. It's widely praised for its engaging gameplay, easy-to-learn mechanics, and immersive VR experience.

Why Unreal Engine for Beat Saber:

- **Real-Time Visuals**: *Beat Saber* features vibrant, fast-paced visuals that change dynamically based on the music. Unreal Engine's real-time rendering capabilities were key in achieving these effects.

- **Responsive Motion**: The game's reliance on fast, precise hand movements is powered by Unreal's motion controller support. Players must sync their movements perfectly with the music, and Unreal Engine ensures that every interaction is smooth and responsive.

- **Cross-Platform Play**: *Beat Saber* is available on multiple VR platforms, including Oculus Rift, HTC Vive, and PlayStation VR. Unreal Engine's cross-platform development tools made it easier to create a consistent experience across various devices.

The success of *Beat Saber* serves as an excellent example of Unreal Engine's capabilities in creating an engaging and highly interactive VR experience, where the engine's graphical power, VR support, and real-time rendering play a critical role.

This chapter provides a solid foundation for understanding game engines, particularly Unreal Engine, and how they play a central role in VR development. By explaining the advantages of Unreal Engine, setting up the development environment, and showcasing a popular VR game, readers are now equipped with the knowledge to begin their own VR development journey.

CHAPTER 3

CORE CONCEPTS IN UNREAL ENGINE

Blueprints and C++: Introduction to Unreal's Visual Scripting System and C++ Integration

Blueprints in Unreal Engine: Unreal Engine offers two primary methods for programming game logic: **Blueprints** (visual scripting) and **C++** (traditional programming). **Blueprints** is Unreal Engine's node-based visual scripting system, designed to make it easier for developers, especially those without extensive programming experience, to create gameplay mechanics, interactions, and logic. Here's an overview of both:

- **Visual Scripting with Blueprints**: Blueprints allow developers to design and implement logic by connecting "nodes" that represent functions, events, and variables. These nodes are visually connected like a flowchart, and once connected, they form the logic behind interactions within the game. For instance, if you want to make a door open when the player approaches, you can create a Blueprint that handles detecting the player's position and triggering the door's movement.

- o **Advantages**:
  - No need to write code: Blueprints are ideal for beginners or developers who prefer not to code.
  - Fast iteration: Changes can be made quickly without recompiling the entire project.
  - Visual feedback: Immediate visualization of game logic helps with debugging and understanding workflows.
- o **Real-World Example**: In a VR game, you might use Blueprints to create interactive objects like a lever or a button. When the player's hand controller overlaps with the object, the Blueprint logic can trigger an animation or a sound effect.
- **C++ in Unreal Engine**: Unreal Engine also supports **C++**, a powerful programming language that allows developers to access the full breadth of the engine's capabilities. While Blueprints are great for prototyping and quick development, C++ offers more performance, flexibility, and control.

- o **Advantages**:
  - Performance: C++ allows for greater optimization and performance, which is critical for VR, where frame rates need to be consistent.
  - Full control: C++ allows for access to the full Unreal Engine API, giving developers complete control over the game mechanics.
  - Reusability and maintainability: C++ code is modular, making it easier to scale and reuse across different projects.
- o **Real-World Example**: Suppose you want to create a custom AI behavior for a character in VR. While Blueprints can handle basic behaviors, using C++ will allow you to optimize the logic for high-performance needs, such as pathfinding, movement, and decision-making, ensuring it runs smoothly in VR environments.

Blueprints vs. C++: Both Blueprints and C++ can be used together in Unreal Engine, with Blueprints handling high level gameplay mechanics and C++ handling performance-critical systems. This hybrid approach allows developers to use the best of both worlds. Many developers start with Blueprints for rapid prototyping and later switch to C++ to optimize and refine their code.

Navigating the Unreal Editor: Overview of the Unreal Engine Interface

The **Unreal Engine Editor** is where developers spend most of their time building, testing, and fine-tuning their projects. It has a rich, multi-window interface designed to give developers access to all the tools they need. Here's a breakdown of the main components of the Unreal Editor interface:

1. **The Viewport**:
   o This is the main window where you see your game world. The **Viewport** allows you to view and interact with your scene in 3D space. You can move around, place objects, and see how changes affect the game in real-time.
   o In VR development, the Viewport is particularly useful for testing scene layouts, object placements, and ensuring that everything is scaled properly for virtual environments.
2. **Content Browser**:
   o The **Content Browser** is where all your assets are stored. This includes textures, models, blueprints, sounds, and more. The Content Browser allows

you to manage and organize these assets for use in your project.

- o For VR, this section is crucial because you will likely need to manage a variety of assets like 3D models, animations, and sound files, which are all essential for creating an immersive VR environment.

3. **Toolbar**:

- o The **Toolbar** at the top of the editor provides quick access to common actions like playing the game, saving your project, and compiling code. It's an essential part of navigating the editor efficiently.
- o In VR development, the **Play In VR** button allows you to instantly test your scene in VR mode, simulating how it would feel for a user to interact with the environment.

4. **World Outliner**:

- o The **World Outliner** is where all the objects in your scene are listed. This helps you manage and organize objects in your VR world, making it easy to select and modify them.
- o For a VR scene, you might see things like the player's VR camera, interactive objects, and environmental assets listed in the World Outliner.

5. **Details Panel**:

o The **Details Panel** displays properties and settings for the selected object in the scene. Whether it's a light, a camera, or an interactive object, the Details Panel allows you to tweak the object's properties, such as position, rotation, scale, and any custom attributes.

o In VR development, this is useful when adjusting properties like the scale of interactive objects to ensure they feel appropriately sized in virtual space.

6. **Blueprint Editor**:

o The **Blueprint Editor** is where you create and edit Blueprints. This node-based editor allows you to design gameplay logic visually. For VR, this is where you'll create interactions like grabbing objects, teleporting, and activating switches.

7. **Viewport Controls**:

o To navigate through the scene, you can use the **viewport controls**. These allow you to move, rotate, and zoom in the editor's 3D space, similar to how you would navigate in a 3D modeling application.

Real-World Example: A Simple VR Scene Created Using Both Blueprints and C++

Scenario:

Let's walk through a simple VR scene where the player can interact with an object (e.g., a door), and upon pressing a button, the door opens, revealing another part of the environment.

1. **Step 1: Setting Up the Scene**:
   o Begin by creating a basic VR environment. This includes placing objects like a door, a button, and walls to frame the environment.
   o In the **Content Browser**, import or create 3D models for the door and button. These assets will be placed in the scene.
   o Set the camera to the player's VR headset, ensuring the player can look around the room.
2. **Step 2: Blueprint Interaction**:
   o **Blueprint for Button Interaction**: Create a **Blueprint** for the button that detects when the player's VR controller is near it. You can do this by adding a **Trigger Box** that activates when the player's hand enters it.
   o **Button Press Logic**: In the **Blueprint Editor**, set up a visual script that, when the player interacts with the button (e.g., pressing it), will trigger the

door to open. This could be done by changing the **rotation** of the door to make it swing open.

3. **Step 3: C++ for Performance Optimization**:
   - While Blueprints handle the high-level interaction, **C++** can be used for performance optimization, such as improving the button's detection system or handling the physics of the door's movement more efficiently.
   - For example, use C++ to create a custom class that handles the door's behavior when it opens or closes. This can include adjusting the door's **speed, acceleration**, and **friction** to make it move more smoothly in the VR world.

4. **Step 4: Testing in VR**:
   - After implementing the Blueprint and C++ logic, test the scene in **VR Mode** by clicking **Play in VR**. Put on your VR headset and check if the interactions work as expected.
   - Ensure that the door responds when the button is pressed, and make adjustments to both the Blueprint logic and C++ code if needed for smooth performance.

This chapter introduces key Unreal Engine concepts like **Blueprints** and **C++**, essential for VR development. It also guides you through the Unreal Editor interface, equipping you with the tools necessary to build and manage your VR world effectively. Finally, by combining both Blueprints and C++, you can create simple yet functional VR interactions while ensuring your game runs efficiently in virtual environments.

CHAPTER 4

INTRODUCTION TO VR HARDWARE

VR Headsets: Overview of Major VR Headsets

Virtual Reality headsets are the gateway to the immersive world of VR. These devices display stereoscopic 3D visuals and track the user's head movements, enabling them to experience the virtual world as if they were physically present. Different headsets are designed for various use cases, from gaming to professional applications. Here's an overview of some of the most popular VR headsets:

1. **Oculus Rift**:
   o **Platform**: PC-based VR.
   o **Features**: The Oculus Rift offers high-quality VR experiences with precise positional tracking via external sensors. It includes a pair of hand controllers that allow users to interact with virtual environments.
   o **Pros**: Great visual quality, powerful PC integration, and reliable tracking.

    o **Cons**: Requires a PC with significant processing power, and the setup can be cumbersome with external sensors.

2. **HTC Vive**:

    o **Platform**: PC-based VR.

    o **Features**: The HTC Vive uses external base stations for precise 6DoF (six degrees of freedom) tracking, allowing users to move around in large spaces. It's known for its immersive experiences, including room-scale VR, where users can walk freely in their virtual environments.

    o **Pros**: Excellent tracking accuracy, room-scale VR, and strong developer support.

    o **Cons**: Requires a high-end PC and external sensors, which may be expensive and require setup space.

3. **PlayStation VR (PSVR)**:

    o **Platform**: Console-based VR (PlayStation 4/5).

    o **Features**: PSVR connects to the PlayStation console, making it more accessible for console gamers. It uses the PlayStation Camera for tracking and comes with the PlayStation Move controllers for interaction.

    o **Pros**: Affordable compared to PC VR headsets, great for PlayStation users.

o **Cons**: Lower resolution compared to PC VR headsets, limited to PlayStation ecosystem.

4. **Oculus Quest and Quest 2**:

   o **Platform**: Standalone VR (no need for PC or console).

   o **Features**: The Oculus Quest and Quest 2 are wireless standalone VR headsets, meaning they don't need to be connected to a computer or console. The Oculus Quest 2, in particular, offers excellent performance for its price, with the ability to run fully immersive VR experiences right out of the box.

   o **Pros**: Wireless freedom, no PC required, easy to set up, and relatively affordable.

   o **Cons**: Limited graphics capabilities compared to PC VR headsets, shorter battery life.

5. **Valve Index**:

   o **Platform**: PC-based VR.

   o **Features**: The Valve Index is known for its high refresh rate (up to 144Hz) and high-quality optics, making it a top choice for enthusiasts seeking the best visual experience in VR. It also features the finger-tracking **Index Controllers**, which offer a more immersive experience by tracking individual finger movements.

- o **Pros**: Top-tier visuals, excellent comfort, and precision tracking with the Index Controllers.
- o **Cons**: Expensive and requires a powerful PC.

Controllers and Tracking Systems: How Controllers, Sensors, and Haptic Feedback Work

To fully interact with VR environments, VR headsets are paired with specialized controllers and tracking systems that detect user input and respond in real-time. The key components that contribute to this interactive experience include:

1. **Motion Controllers**:
   - o **Function**: Motion controllers allow users to interact with virtual objects, navigate menus, and manipulate their environment. These controllers track the user's hand movements, providing a direct and intuitive way to interact with the virtual world.
   - o **Example**: The **Oculus Touch** controllers for the Oculus Rift and Oculus Quest allow for motion tracking, button inputs, and gestures, providing a lifelike experience where users can reach out, grab objects, and perform actions.
   - o **Types**:

- **Tracked Controllers**: These use sensors to track the position of the controllers relative to the VR headset. Examples include the HTC Vive controllers and the PlayStation Move controllers.
- **Hand Tracking**: More advanced headsets like the Oculus Quest 2 are introducing hand tracking, which allows users to interact with the virtual world without physical controllers. The system uses cameras built into the headset to track the hands, offering a more natural experience.

2. **Tracking Systems**:
   - **External Sensors**: Some VR systems, like the HTC Vive, rely on external base stations (also known as lighthouses) to track the position of both the headset and controllers. These stations emit infrared signals that the headset and controllers pick up, allowing for 6DoF tracking.
   - **Inside-Out Tracking**: Headsets like the Oculus Quest and Rift S use **inside-out tracking**, where cameras embedded in the headset detect the environment and track the position of the user in the room without requiring external sensors.

o **Positional Tracking**: This refers to the ability of the system to track movement in three-dimensional space (forward/backward, up/down, left/right). 6DoF (Six Degrees of Freedom) enables full movement tracking, making users feel like they are physically in the virtual world.

3. **Haptic Feedback**:

o **Function**: Haptic feedback involves the use of vibrations or forces in the controllers or headset to simulate the feeling of physical interactions. For instance, when a user touches a virtual object or receives a blow in a VR game, the controller will vibrate, simulating the sensation.

o **Purpose**: Haptic feedback adds an extra layer of immersion, making the virtual world feel more tactile. It can also help simulate the weight of objects, the sensation of grabbing or pressing something, or even simulate environmental interactions (such as feeling the vibration of footsteps on different surfaces).

o **Example**: The **Oculus Touch controllers** are equipped with haptic feedback motors that provide varied vibrations to simulate the feeling of physical actions, such as a strong vibration when you hit an object or a light buzz when pressing buttons.

Real-World Example: The Impact of Wireless Technology on VR (Oculus Quest 2)

The **Oculus Quest 2** represents a significant advancement in VR hardware, primarily because of its **wireless** design. Unlike previous VR headsets, which required external sensors or a connected PC, the Oculus Quest 2 is a fully standalone device that works without the need for wires, making VR more accessible, portable, and user-friendly. Here's how the wireless technology impacts the VR experience:

1. **Freedom of Movement**: The Oculus Quest 2 allows users to experience VR without being tethered to a computer. This freedom removes the constraints of cables, allowing users to move around freely in a room-scale VR environment. This is especially important for immersive experiences where users need to walk, jump, or interact with objects in the virtual world.

2. **Ease of Setup**: With the Oculus Quest 2, users no longer need to set up external base stations or connect to a powerful gaming PC. All you need is the headset and a room to play in. The setup is as simple as putting on the headset and setting up a play area using the built-in software. This simplicity is a game-changer for casual users and developers alike.

3. **Performance vs. Standalone Limitations**: While the wireless nature of the Quest 2 provides more flexibility, it does come with some limitations in terms of performance. Since the headset doesn't rely on a PC, it uses an internal processor, which can't match the raw power of a dedicated gaming computer. This means that the graphics and complexity of VR experiences may be less advanced than those seen on high-end PC-based headsets like the HTC Vive or Valve Index.

4. **Wireless PC VR (Air Link)**: The Oculus Quest 2 also supports **Air Link**, which allows users to wirelessly stream VR content from a PC to the Quest 2, effectively combining the best of both worlds. You get the wireless freedom of a standalone device, along with the enhanced performance of a PC VR headset when you need it. This feature opens the door to a wider range of VR experiences without the need for cumbersome cables.

Conclusion:

The Oculus Quest 2 is a prime example of how wireless technology is transforming VR. It has helped to democratize virtual reality by making it more affordable, portable, and easier to use. As wireless technology continues to evolve, we can expect even more advancements in VR hardware, making it more immersive, accessible, and user-friendly than ever before.

This chapter has introduced the key hardware components of virtual reality, from headsets and controllers to tracking systems and wireless technology. Understanding these elements is essential for developing VR experiences that are both immersive and user-friendly. By exploring real-world examples like the Oculus Quest 2, you can see firsthand how VR hardware continues to evolve and improve the overall user experience.

CHAPTER 5

SETTING UP A VR PROJECT IN UNREAL ENGINE

Starting a VR Project: Step-by-Step Guide to Creating a New VR Project

Creating a VR project in Unreal Engine is straightforward, especially with the tools and templates provided by the engine. Whether you're just beginning or you're looking to optimize your development workflow, Unreal Engine offers everything you need to get started with VR development. Here's how to set up your own VR project:

1. **Step 1: Install Unreal Engine**
   - If you haven't already, download and install Unreal Engine through the **Epic Games Launcher**. Make sure to install the latest version of Unreal Engine (e.g., Unreal 4.x or Unreal 5.x), as the newer versions offer improved VR support.

2. **Step 2: Open the Unreal Engine Launcher**
   - After installation, open the **Epic Games Launcher** and launch Unreal Engine. The first

screen you see will allow you to choose between existing projects or create a new one.

3. **Step 3: Select a New Project**
   - To start a new project, click on the **New Project** tab.
   - Select **Games** under the "Project Categories."
   - Then choose the **Blank** template. This gives you the flexibility to build a custom VR experience without predefined game logic or assets.

4. **Step 4: Configure Project Settings**
   - **Blueprint or C++**: Decide whether you want to use Blueprints or C++ for development. If you're new to programming, it's recommended to choose **Blueprints**, as it allows for rapid prototyping without the need for coding.
   - **With Starter Content**: Choose to include **Starter Content** if you want basic assets like textures, meshes, and materials to help you get started quickly. For a simple VR project, you can skip this step to keep the project minimal.

5. **Step 5: Set the Project's Output Settings**
   - Choose whether your VR project will be for **Windows** or another platform. Unreal Engine supports PC VR, mobile VR, and console VR development, but the most common for development is **Windows**.

- o Name your project (e.g., "VR_Project") and choose a directory where it will be saved. Click **Create**.

6. **Step 6: Set Up VR Support in Unreal**
   - o After creating the project, go to **Edit** > **Project Settings** > **Engine** > **Input** to enable VR-specific input and action mappings (e.g., hand controllers, movement input).
   - o Ensure the project is configured to run in **VR Mode** by checking **VR Plugins** (Oculus, HTC Vive, etc.) and enabling the proper settings for your target platform.

7. **Step 7: Test the Project in VR**
   - o Once the project is set up, you can test it in VR by pressing **Play** and selecting **VR Preview** from the dropdown options.
   - o Put on your VR headset to see the results. You should see a basic environment (such as a simple 3D world) where you can interact with objects using your VR controllers.

VR Template: How to Use Unreal's VR Template

Unreal Engine provides a **VR Template** that offers a great starting point for VR development. This template includes pre-configured interactions and input systems, so you can focus on creating your content rather than setting up the basics of VR interaction. Here's how to use it:

1. **Step 1: Create a New VR Project Using the VR Template**
   - When you launch the Unreal Engine and go to the **New Project** screen, select **Games** again.
   - This time, choose the **Virtual Reality** template from the list of available templates.
   - Select **With Starter Content** to include a basic set of assets, or choose **No Starter Content** if you want a clean slate.

2. **Step 2: Explore the VR Template**
   - The VR Template includes several key components:
     - **VR Pawn**: A pre-configured blueprint that handles head and controller tracking.
     - **VR Controllers**: Blueprints that allow interaction with the environment, including the ability to grab, throw, and manipulate objects.
     - **VR Camera**: A VR-specific camera that simulates the player's head movements and adjusts the field of view based on their position.

3. **Step 3: Review the Default VR Interaction System**

- o Unreal's VR Template includes basic interaction systems for VR controllers. It allows for picking up, throwing, and interacting with objects, which is ideal for building immersive VR applications.
- o Open the **Blueprints** for the VR Pawn to customize how your VR character moves, grabs, and interacts with the virtual world.

4. **Step 4: Customize the Template**
   - o From this point, you can modify the project to suit your needs:
     - **Add Objects**: Place interactive objects, NPCs, or environments in the scene.
     - **Edit Interactions**: Adjust the existing interactions in the VR Pawn blueprint or add your own custom VR mechanics using Blueprints.

5. **Step 5: Testing and Refining**
   - o Use **VR Preview** to test the VR interactions and scene performance in real-time.
   - o You can quickly iterate on your VR project by tweaking the settings, adding new assets, or modifying Blueprints.

Real-World Example: Creating a Basic Room-Scale VR Environment

Let's walk through the process of creating a **basic room-scale VR environment** using Unreal Engine's VR Template. This example will guide you in setting up a simple virtual room where users can interact with objects in a VR space.

1. **Step 1: Set Up the Environment**
   - Start by creating a new project using the **VR Template** as described above.
   - In the **Content Browser**, find the **Starter Content** folder. Drag and drop a few basic assets, such as walls, a floor, and a ceiling, to create a simple room. You can scale these assets to create a room with enough space for the user to move around.

2. **Step 2: Implement the VR Interaction System**
   - The VR Template includes a basic interaction system, but let's add a few more elements to enhance the experience:
     - **Add a Table**: Place a table in the center of the room.
     - **Add Objects to the Table**: Add a few simple interactive objects, such as a ball or a cube.
     - **Blueprint for Interactions**: Open the **VR Pawn** Blueprint and adjust the

54

interaction logic to allow the player to pick up and move the objects on the table using their controllers.

3. **Step 3: Test the Environment in VR**

   o Once your environment is set up, test the scene in VR mode. Put on your headset and check that you can walk around the room and interact with the objects.

   o Make sure the interaction feels smooth. The objects should respond to your hand movements, and you should be able to pick them up and place them in different areas of the room.

4. **Step 4: Refining the Experience**

   o Adjust the size and placement of objects to ensure that everything is appropriately scaled for room-scale VR.

   o You can also add additional features, such as sound effects (e.g., footsteps, ambient noise), to enhance immersion.

   o Experiment with different lighting setups and post-processing effects to create the desired atmosphere for your room.

This chapter provided a clear, step-by-step guide on how to start a new VR project in Unreal Engine, use the VR template, and create a basic room-scale VR environment. Whether you are working on a simple interactive experience or an intricate VR game, Unreal Engine's tools, including the VR Template, make it easy to begin creating immersive virtual environments. The VR template's built-in interactions and customizable features will save you valuable development time, allowing you to focus on creating unique and engaging experiences for your users.

CHAPTER 6

VR MOTION AND INTERACTION BASICS

Hand Tracking and Movement: Setting Up Basic Motion Controls

Hand tracking and movement are essential components of creating an immersive VR experience. VR motion controls allow users to interact with their virtual environment using hand gestures, controller movements, and physical movement. Setting up motion controls in Unreal Engine involves configuring both the head tracking (which controls the user's viewpoint) and the hand controllers (which allow interaction with objects).

1. **Step 1: Enable Motion Controller Support**
   - First, ensure that your VR project in Unreal Engine is set up with the appropriate VR hardware (e.g., Oculus Rift, HTC Vive, Oculus Quest). Unreal Engine's **VR Template** automatically supports motion controllers for popular VR systems.
   - Go to **Edit** > **Project Settings** > **Engine** > **Input** to enable motion controller input.

o Assign the actions for your motion controllers. Typically, motion controllers will use inputs such as **Trigger**, **Grip**, and **Thumbstick**.

2. **Step 2: Setting Up Motion Controller Blueprints**

o In the **VR Template**, motion controllers are preconfigured to track the player's hands in space. You can find these Blueprints in the **VR Pawn**.

o You can modify the **VR Pawn Blueprint** to adjust how the motion controllers react within the game. For example, you can add logic to detect the position and rotation of the controllers, ensuring that the user's hand movements are accurately represented in the virtual world.

3. **Step 3: Adding Basic Movement Controls**

o For movement, most VR games use two types of locomotion: **teleportation** and **smooth locomotion**.

▪ **Teleportation**: Teleportation allows users to quickly move from one location to another in the VR world by pointing to a destination and pressing a button (typically the thumbstick or trigger).

▪ **Smooth Locomotion**: Smooth locomotion allows continuous movement through the environment, which can be controlled by thumbstick input. This method requires special consideration for comfort to avoid motion sickness.

- o Unreal Engine supports both of these locomotion methods, which can be configured in the **VR Pawn** Blueprint.

4. **Step 4: Test Hand Tracking in VR**

- o After setting up the controllers and movement controls, test the hand tracking by launching the **VR Preview** in the Unreal Engine editor. Put on your VR headset, and ensure the motion controllers follow your hand movements correctly.

- o You should see the hands in VR represented by your motion controllers, and you should be able to interact with the environment by moving, grabbing, and pointing.

Interaction Mechanics: Picking Up Objects, Teleportation, and Grabbing

In VR, user interaction with the environment is a critical part of creating a fun and engaging experience. The basic interaction mechanics such as picking up objects, grabbing them, and teleporting—are key to building immersive VR applications. Let's break down how to implement these interactions:

1. **Picking Up and Grabbing Objects**
   o In the **VR Template**, interaction with objects is already set up using Blueprints. For example, when the user presses the grip button on their motion controller, they can grab an object in the environment.
   o **Step 1: Create an Interactable Object**:
     ▪ In Unreal Engine, objects that can be picked up or interacted with should have **Collision Components** enabled. For example, a cube that can be grabbed should have a **Box Collision** component attached to it.
     ▪ Set the object's collision settings to **Overlap** to allow the player's hand or controller to "touch" it.
   o **Step 2: Blueprint Logic for Grabbing**:
     ▪ In the **VR Pawn Blueprint**, add the logic for detecting when the player's controller overlaps with the object. This can be done using the **On Component Begin Overlap** node to detect when the controller enters the object's collision area.
     ▪ Once the object is grabbed (via the grip button), you can attach it to the

controller's position. The **Attach Actor to Component** node is typically used for this.

- When the grip button is released, you can detach the object from the controller and place it in the virtual environment at its new position.

2. **Teleportation**
   o Teleportation is an essential movement mechanic in VR that reduces the chances of motion sickness while allowing users to quickly explore the environment.

   o **Step 1: Setting Up Teleportation**:
     - Unreal Engine's **VR Template** comes with built-in teleportation logic that allows users to teleport by pointing to a location in the environment and pressing a button.
     - You can modify the teleportation logic in the **VR Pawn** Blueprint to change how far users can teleport, how the teleportation arc is displayed, and the appearance of the teleportation marker (usually an arc showing the intended destination).

   o **Step 2: Testing Teleportation**:

61

- Once configured, you can test teleportation by using the **VR Preview** mode. When you press the designated teleportation button on the motion controller, the player should be able to point to a location on the floor and instantly teleport to that spot.

3. **Grabbing Objects (Advanced Interaction)**:
   o More complex interactions, such as throwing or dropping objects, can be set up similarly. When the user releases the object (by releasing the grip button), you can apply a force or velocity to simulate throwing the object. This is achieved using **Add Force** or **Launch Projectile** nodes in Blueprints.

Real-World Example: Interactive VR Object Manipulation in a Simple Puzzle Game

Let's consider a simple puzzle game where the player must grab and manipulate objects to solve puzzles. The game's goal is to stack a set of objects to reach a button that opens a door. Here's how you would implement basic object manipulation and interaction mechanics for this type of puzzle game:

1. **Step 1: Design the Puzzle Environment**

- o Create a basic environment where the puzzle will take place. For example, place a table, a stack of cubes, and a door that remains locked until the player completes the puzzle.
- o Add a **Button** near the door that is activated when the player stacks the cubes in a specific configuration.

2. **Step 2: Implement Object Interactions**
    - o **Create Interactable Objects**: Make each cube or object interactable by attaching collision components (e.g., Box Collision) and enabling **Overlap** events.
    - o **Grabbing Logic**: Set up Blueprint logic to detect when the player's controller overlaps with the cube. When the player presses the grip button, the object should attach to the controller. You can use the **Attach Actor to Component** node to lock the cube to the player's hand.
    - o **Drop Logic**: When the player releases the cube, it should drop to the ground, or you can apply a small force to simulate a more natural release.

3. **Step 3: Implement Teleportation**
    - o Allow the player to move around the environment quickly by setting up teleportation. Place teleportation markers on the ground, and use the thumbstick or trigger to activate teleportation.

- o Teleportation will help the player easily move around the puzzle space without discomfort, allowing them to adjust their position when stacking objects.

4. **Step 4: Puzzle Logic**
   - o **Button Interaction**: Once the player stacks the cubes correctly on the designated platform near the door, trigger the button press by using a **Collision** event when the cubes touch the button.
   - o **Unlock the Door**: When the button is pressed (cubes stacked correctly), use Blueprint logic to open the door by changing the door's position (using the **Set Actor Location** or **Open Animation**).

5. **Step 5: Testing the Game**
   - o Once the interaction system is set up, test the puzzle game in **VR Preview** mode. Put on your headset, and try grabbing, moving, and stacking the cubes. Ensure that the interaction feels smooth and natural.
   - o Check the teleportation system to make sure the player can easily navigate the puzzle area.

This chapter provides a foundation for understanding and implementing basic motion and interaction mechanics in VR using Unreal Engine. By mastering hand tracking, object manipulation, and teleportation, you can create more engaging and immersive VR experiences. The real-world example of a simple puzzle game demonstrates how these systems come together to form the core of many VR games, offering an intuitive way for players to interact with the virtual world.

CHAPTER 7

ADVANCED VR MOVEMENT TECHNIQUES

Locomotion Methods: Teleportation vs. Walking, Smooth Locomotion, and Comfort Options

In virtual reality (VR), locomotion—the way the player moves through the virtual world—is one of the most critical aspects of design. How players navigate in VR has a significant impact on their immersion, comfort, and overall experience. There are several locomotion methods, each with its strengths and drawbacks. Let's dive into the most common ones.

1. **Teleportation**:

    o **Description**: Teleportation allows players to move quickly from one spot to another by pointing to a location in the game world and "teleporting" there instantly. This method is designed to avoid motion sickness, as it eliminates the visual conflict between the player's movement and their stationary body.

    o **Advantages**:

- **Comfort**: Teleportation is the most comfortable locomotion method for most users because it avoids continuous movement, reducing the risk of motion sickness.
- **Fast and Efficient**: It allows users to traverse large environments quickly and with minimal physical effort.

o **Disadvantages**:

- **Limited Immersion**: Teleportation can break the feeling of immersion, as players can't physically walk or run in the virtual space. It feels less natural compared to real movement.
- **Disorienting in Some Cases**: Some users may still experience disorientation when teleporting, especially if the destination causes a drastic change in the environment's layout.

2. **Walking and Room-Scale Movement**:

o **Description**: In room-scale VR, players move by physically walking around within the boundaries of their play area. This method offers the most natural and immersive form of locomotion, as it mirrors real-life movement.

o **Advantages**:

- **Natural**: Walking in VR feels intuitive, and it enhances immersion by making players feel like they are physically present in the virtual environment.
- **Full Range of Motion**: It allows players to interact more naturally with their surroundings by simply moving around.

o **Disadvantages**:

- **Limited Space**: Players are confined to the physical space available in their play area. For large virtual worlds, this can feel restrictive, and it's not suitable for environments larger than the player's available space.
- **Physical Strain**: Walking in place or constantly moving may cause fatigue, especially if the VR session lasts for an extended period.

3. **Smooth Locomotion**:

o **Description**: Smooth locomotion allows for continuous movement in the virtual world, using the thumbstick or touchpad on the controller. This method closely mimics the walking or running experience in traditional games.

o **Advantages**:

- **Full Movement Freedom**: Smooth locomotion provides continuous freedom of movement, allowing players to travel as far and as fast as needed without limitations of space.
- **Immersion**: It's more immersive than teleportation because it simulates real-world motion, making it ideal for action-oriented VR games.

o **Disadvantages**:

- **Motion Sickness Risk**: Smooth locomotion can cause discomfort and nausea for some users, as the brain receives conflicting signals: it thinks the body is moving but the eyes show no movement.
- **Potential for Disorientation**: Without additional comfort features, smooth locomotion may cause dizziness, especially in fast-paced or complex VR environments.

4. **Comfort Options for Locomotion**:

o **Snap Turning**: Instead of rotating continuously with smooth motion, players can turn by "snapping" to 30 or 45-degree increments. This helps reduce the disorientation associated with continuous movement.

- o **Blurring/Field of View (FOV) Reduction**: Many VR games reduce the FOV or apply a blur effect when moving to limit the sense of motion sickness. The FOV narrows during movement to reduce the peripheral vision effect.
- o **Speed Adjustment**: Allowing players to adjust the speed of their locomotion can help avoid discomfort. Lowering the movement speed or offering a "comfort mode" can make smooth locomotion more tolerable.

Handling Motion Sickness: Best Practices to Reduce VR Nausea

Motion sickness is one of the most significant barriers to VR adoption, especially for experiences involving fast movement or smooth locomotion. However, there are several best practices to minimize nausea and discomfort:

1. **Frame Rate and Latency**:
   - o A steady frame rate is essential for reducing VR nausea. Aim for at least **90 FPS**, as lower frame rates can lead to a mismatch between the user's head movements and the frame rendering, causing motion sickness.

o **Reduce Latency**: Minimize input and rendering latency, which can disrupt the player's sense of presence and induce nausea.

2. **Comfortable Locomotion**:

   o As discussed earlier, **Teleportation** and **Snap Turning** are generally the most comfortable methods for movement. These prevent users from experiencing the motion sickness associated with continuous movement.

   o **Vary the Speed of Movement**: Avoid fast, sudden movements in VR. Let users control the speed of their motion to help them maintain comfort during gameplay.

3. **Field of View (FOV) Adjustment**:

   o **Reduce Peripheral Vision**: Use FOV adjustments to narrow the user's peripheral vision during movement. This reduces the visual disparity between what the brain expects and what it sees, which helps in preventing nausea.

   o **Blurring Effects**: Applying a blur or a vignette effect around the edges of the screen during movement can also help reduce nausea, as it focuses the user's attention on the center of the screen.

4. **Physical Comfort**:

o Ensure that the VR headset is positioned comfortably on the player's head, with the lens set at the correct eye distance. Discomfort from improper headset fit can increase the likelihood of motion sickness.

o **Take Breaks**: Encourage users to take regular breaks during VR sessions. Shorter playtimes reduce the chance of nausea, allowing players to recover and resume play without discomfort.

5. **User Feedback**:

o Many VR games now include options to adjust comfort settings, such as turning on **comfort mode**, which lowers the movement speed or adjusts the FOV during intense moments.

o **Personalization**: Allow players to customize settings like motion speed, snap turn angles, and FOV reduction based on their preferences.

Real-World Example: Walking Simulation in a VR Nature Experience

A great example of using advanced VR movement techniques is a **VR nature simulation** game. Imagine a VR experience where users are immersed in a virtual forest, walking along trails, interacting with wildlife, and exploring natural environments.

Here's how advanced locomotion techniques can be applied to enhance the experience:

1. **Walking Simulation with Room-Scale Movement**:
   o The game can be designed for **room-scale VR**, where users walk around a simulated forest environment, exploring areas like forests, lakes, and mountains.
   o **Room-Scale Interaction**: Players physically walk around their play area, with the game tracking their movements and allowing them to explore the virtual space freely. This method offers the most natural and immersive experience, as it mirrors real-world walking.
   o **Environmental Interaction**: As players walk through the forest, they can interact with plants, touch trees, or sit by the riverbank. This interaction would rely on the natural movements of the player's hands and body.

2. **Smooth Locomotion for Virtual Exploration**:
   o For areas beyond the player's physical play space, smooth locomotion is used. Players can use the thumbstick to move across the virtual terrain, providing a seamless exploration experience. The speed of locomotion can be adjusted to suit the player's comfort level.

- o **Comfort Settings**: The game can implement **snap turning** and **FOV reduction** while moving to ensure that users who experience motion sickness can enjoy the experience comfortably.

3. **Teleportation for Long-Distance Travel**:
   - o If players wish to quickly move to distant areas within the forest or across the mountain range, teleportation is used. Players can point to the desired location and teleport instantly, which minimizes the risk of nausea associated with continuous movement.
   - o **Interactive Travel**: When a player teleports to a distant area, the game could simulate the feeling of moving through a transition, such as a brief fade-out and fade-in effect, enhancing the feeling of travel while maintaining immersion.

4. **Handling Motion Sickness in the Nature Experience**:
   - o The natural pace of walking in a VR nature experience reduces motion sickness, as it feels very intuitive. However, for users sensitive to smooth locomotion, **snap-turning** and **FOV narrowing** can be implemented to further reduce discomfort.
   - o Environmental cues like **sound** (birds chirping, water flowing) and **ambient effects** (wind,

rustling leaves) further enhance immersion, keeping the player grounded in the virtual world.

This chapter covered advanced movement techniques and methods to improve comfort and immersion in VR experiences. By incorporating smooth locomotion, teleportation, and comfort options, VR developers can cater to a wider audience, ensuring that their experiences are enjoyable and accessible to all players. The real-world example of a walking simulation in a nature experience demonstrates how these techniques can be applied to create seamless, immersive VR environments that are both comfortable and engaging.

CHAPTER 8

DEVELOPING IMMERSIVE VR ENVIRONMENTS

3D Asset Creation for VR: How to Create Assets Optimized for VR

Creating 3D assets for VR is fundamentally different from creating assets for traditional 3D games or other media. In VR, the assets must not only look realistic but also be optimized for real-time rendering to ensure that the experience runs smoothly and comfortably. VR environments require a high level of detail, but also optimization to ensure that the frame rate stays high and the experience remains immersive.

1. **Polygon Count and Complexity**:
   o **Low-Poly Models**: High-polygon models can be extremely taxing on VR systems, so it's essential to create **low-poly models** for VR. These models should contain as few polygons as possible while still maintaining visual quality.
   o **Optimizing Geometry**: Use techniques like **level of detail (LOD)**, which adjusts the complexity of models based on their distance from the camera. Objects closer to the player should have more

detail, while distant objects can use simpler, lower-poly versions.

- o **Avoid Overdetailed Objects**: For objects that won't be closely inspected (such as background elements), keep the detail level low. Focus on making the main interactable or visible assets more detailed.

2. **Texture Optimization**:
   - o **Use Atlas Textures**: A texture atlas allows multiple textures to be combined into a single image file. This reduces the number of texture calls during rendering, which can significantly improve performance.
   - o **Efficient UV Mapping**: Proper **UV mapping** ensures that textures are applied efficiently, reducing any potential seams or distortions that could break immersion in VR. Use **tiling textures** or procedural textures when possible to further reduce texture file sizes.
   - o **Compression**: Use texture compression formats such as **DDS** (DirectDraw Surface) or **PVR** (PowerVR) to reduce texture memory usage without sacrificing quality.

3. **Lighting and Material Considerations**:
   - o **Baked Lighting**: For static objects that don't change (such as the environment), **baked**

lighting can be used to precompute lighting and shadows, reducing the real-time processing load. Unreal Engine provides a powerful **lightmap baking** tool for this purpose.

- o **Efficient Shaders**: For VR, shaders need to be optimized to maintain performance while still providing realistic visuals. Use simple shaders for background objects and more complex shaders for interactable or important assets.

4. **Testing for Performance**:

- o VR requires a steady frame rate, typically **90 FPS or higher**. Regularly test your 3D models and assets in the actual VR environment to ensure that your scene maintains the desired performance. Pay attention to how your scene looks and feels when you run it in VR mode.

5. **Real-Time Asset Creation for VR**:

- o Use tools such as **Unreal Engine's native modeler** or integrate external software like **Blender**, **Maya**, or **3ds Max** to create assets. When importing assets into Unreal, make sure to optimize them for real-time performance by using the appropriate export settings.

Lighting and Shadows in VR: Realistic Lighting and Shadow Effects

Lighting plays a crucial role in making VR environments look realistic and immersive. However, because VR requires high performance, special care must be taken to balance realistic lighting with performance considerations.

1. **Types of Lighting in Unreal Engine**:
   - o **Dynamic Lighting**: Dynamic lights change in real time based on the environment or user actions. For example, a moving object may cast changing shadows depending on the direction of the light. While dynamic lighting adds realism, it can be performance-intensive.
   - o **Static Lighting**: Static lights are precomputed and don't change during gameplay, which is perfect for objects that don't move or interact. **Baked lighting** is an example of static lighting, and it's often used for static meshes or background elements to save on performance.
   - o **Stationary Lighting**: Stationary lights allow for real-time adjustments but have limitations. They provide a good compromise between static and dynamic lighting, particularly in areas where you don't need to have lights constantly changing but still want some flexibility.
2. **Lighting Optimization for VR**:

- o **Use Lightmaps for Static Objects**: Lightmaps are precomputed textures that store lighting information. They can be applied to static objects in your scene, saving on real-time calculations. Unreal Engine's **lightmass** system handles this process.

- o **Shadow Optimization**: Shadows can be computationally expensive in VR. To optimize shadows:
    - Use **lower resolution shadow maps** for distant objects.
    - Use **cascaded shadow maps** (CSM) for real-time shadows, which break the shadow into multiple levels based on distance, keeping close objects sharp and distant objects soft.
    - Consider using **shadow bias** techniques to reduce shadow artifacts such as "shadow acne" or "Peter Panning" (the visual effects that occur when shadows are incorrectly projected).

3. **Lighting Effects**:
    - o **Ambient Occlusion (AO)**: This technique adds realism by darkening creases, holes, and surfaces that are close to each other. However, **Screen-Space Ambient Occlusion (SSAO)** can be

computationally expensive, so **baked AO** or simpler versions of this effect may be more suitable for VR.

- o **Global Illumination (GI)**: Global illumination simulates how light bounces off surfaces in an environment. In Unreal Engine, **Lumen** (Unreal's GI system) helps produce more realistic lighting. However, using it in VR requires careful optimization to avoid hitting performance thresholds.

4. **Post-Processing Effects**:
   - o Post-processing effects such as **bloom, depth of field**, and **color grading** can enhance the visual appeal of a VR scene, but they must be used sparingly in VR to avoid performance hits and prevent discomfort. Some post-processing effects can also cause visual distortion, so they should be tailored to suit the VR experience.

Real-World Example: Developing an Immersive VR Environment for an Architectural Walkthrough

In this example, we'll explore how to develop a simple yet immersive **VR architectural walkthrough**. This type of environment allows users to explore and interact with a 3D model of a building or a room, often used in architecture and real estate.

1. **Step 1: Setting Up the Environment**

   o **Modeling the Building**: Start by creating or importing a 3D model of the building using software like **Revit, Blender, or 3ds Max**. Ensure that all textures and materials are optimized for VR.

   o **Importing Assets**: Import the model into Unreal Engine, paying attention to scale. A key part of making an architectural walkthrough feel realistic is ensuring that the scale of objects feels natural in VR.

2. **Step 2: Applying Lighting and Materials**

   o **Baking Lighting**: For an architectural walkthrough, most of the lighting can be baked using Unreal's **Lightmass** system to ensure that the environment looks well-lit while maintaining high performance.

   o **Adding Lighting Fixtures**: Include static lights such as ceiling lamps or natural lighting through windows. Ensure the lighting is soft and diffuse to mimic real-world illumination.

   o **Realistic Materials**: Use **PBR (Physically Based Rendering)** materials to create realistic textures for walls, floors, and furniture. Materials should have realistic reflections and surface details, but keep textures optimized to avoid unnecessary performance hits.

3. **Step 3: Implementing Motion Controls and Interaction**

   o **Room-Scale Interaction**: Enable **room-scale VR** by setting up the player's VR controls to allow movement through the environment. Players should be able to walk around the space, view the details of the architecture, and even interact with objects (e.g., opening doors, turning on lights).

   o **Teleportation for Long Distances**: Use teleportation as a movement method for long-distance travel between rooms or levels in the building. This will minimize the chances of motion sickness, especially in larger environments.

4. **Step 4: Testing and Refining the Environment**

   o Once the environment is set up, test the scene in **VR Preview** mode. Walk through the building to ensure that the scale feels accurate and the lighting looks realistic.

   o Pay attention to performance—VR needs to run at a steady **90 FPS** or higher to avoid discomfort. If the frame rate drops, consider reducing the number of real-time lights, adjusting the complexity of the model, or simplifying textures.

5. **Step 5: Enhancing Immersion**

   o **Sound Design**: Adding ambient sounds (e.g., footsteps, wind, distant city sounds) can greatly enhance immersion in a VR architectural walkthrough. Use **spatial audio** to make sounds emanate from realistic locations.

   o **Interactive Features**: Allow users to interact with different elements in the environment, such as opening doors or toggling lights on and off. This gives users a sense of control and engagement within the space.

This chapter covered how to create optimized 3D assets and implement realistic lighting and shadows in VR. By focusing on efficiency, realistic materials, and interactive mechanics, you can develop immersive VR environments. The real-world example of an architectural walkthrough demonstrates how these concepts come together to create a fully interactive, visually appealing, and performance-optimized VR experience.

CHAPTER 9

PERFORMANCE OPTIMIZATION FOR VR

Frame Rates and Latency: Importance of Frame Rates in VR for Immersion

In Virtual Reality (VR), achieving a smooth and responsive experience is critical for user immersion and comfort. Frame rates and latency directly influence how comfortable and realistic a VR experience feels.

1. **Importance of Frame Rates in VR**:
    o **Smooth Visuals**: In VR, the goal is to create the sensation of being fully immersed in a digital world. To achieve this, you need a high frame rate, typically **90 frames per second (FPS)** or higher. Frame rates below this threshold can lead to noticeable judder or stuttering, breaking immersion and making users feel disconnected from the virtual world.
    o **Smooth and Continuous Motion**: Frame rates help maintain a continuous flow of movement, which is crucial for avoiding VR-induced motion

sickness. A consistent frame rate reduces the visual discrepancies between head movement and what the eyes are seeing, which is particularly important when users are rotating or moving rapidly through the virtual environment.

o **Reducing Motion Sickness**: In VR, even slight frame drops or delays can disrupt the user's sense of presence and cause discomfort or motion sickness. Keeping the frame rate steady is essential to ensure the experience is comfortable and enjoyable.

2. **Latency and its Impact**:

o **Definition of Latency**: Latency refers to the delay between the user's physical action (such as moving their head or controllers) and the corresponding response in the VR world. Low latency is critical in VR to create a responsive experience.

o **Reducing Latency**: To minimize latency, make sure that all VR devices (headset, controllers, sensors) are well-calibrated and have efficient data transmission. Unreal Engine's **VR template** helps to streamline latency management by handling hardware and input configurations out of the box. Keep latency under **20ms** to ensure a smooth and comfortable experience.

o **Real-Time Rendering**: Unreal Engine uses real-time rendering to ensure that the user's movement in the VR world is tracked instantaneously. However, rendering all the details in a high-fidelity VR environment can be demanding. Efficiently balancing graphical quality and frame rate is essential for low latency and smooth interaction.

3. **Best Practices for Maintaining High Frame Rates**:

o **Consistent 90 FPS**: Always aim for a consistent **90 FPS** for the best VR experience. If your game dips below this, VR users may experience visual artifacts, such as screen tearing or stuttering.

o **Performance Profiling**: Use Unreal Engine's **profiling tools** (e.g., **Unreal Insights** and **GPU Profiler**) to monitor performance and identify areas where optimizations can be made.

Optimizing Assets for VR: Reducing Polygons and Textures for Performance

One of the most important aspects of VR optimization is the efficient use of assets. VR environments often require high levels of detail, but too many complex assets can quickly overwhelm the system's processing power. Here are key strategies for optimizing assets without sacrificing visual quality:

1. **Reducing Polygon Count**:
   o **Low-Poly Models**: In VR, **low-poly models** are crucial to maintain high performance. High-poly models with millions of polygons may look great in traditional games or animations, but they are too taxing for real-time VR rendering. Focus on **reducing polygon count** for non-interactive objects or distant assets.
   o **Level of Detail (LOD)**: Use **Level of Detail (LOD)** models, which automatically swap out high-poly assets for lower-poly versions as they move farther from the camera. This reduces the number of polygons that need to be rendered at any given moment.
   o **Mesh Simplification**: Use tools like **Simplygon** or Unreal's built-in **Mesh Simplifier** to reduce the complexity of 3D models. Keep in mind that simpler meshes don't just help with performance—they also make it easier for the user to interact with the VR environment without overwhelming them with excessive detail.

2. **Texture Optimization**:
   o **Efficient Textures**: Textures play a major role in asset performance. Large, high-resolution textures can take up a lot of memory and processing power, especially in VR. Use

compressed textures where possible and reduce the texture resolution for distant or non-interactive objects.

- **Texture Atlases**: Combine several textures into a **texture atlas** (a large image containing smaller textures). This reduces the number of texture swaps the GPU must make, improving performance.

- **Baked Lighting and Ambient Occlusion**: Instead of using complex real-time lighting, **bake** lighting and shadow effects into the textures themselves. Use **ambient occlusion** (AO) maps to simulate shading in crevices and corners, which enhances realism without the cost of real-time lighting.

- **Unwrap and Optimize UVs**: Properly **unwrap UV maps** and ensure that textures are efficiently applied. Avoid wasted texture space, and use tiling textures for large areas to save on memory.

3. **Optimizing Materials and Shaders**:

- **Simple Shaders**: Complex shaders can reduce performance in VR, so it's important to keep shaders as simple as possible. Use standard **Unreal Engine materials** rather than custom shaders unless necessary.

    o   **Avoid Expensive Effects**: Effects like **real-time reflections, refraction,** and **transparency** can be computationally expensive. Use them sparingly or consider using **baked reflections** and simpler materials.

4. **Instancing and Batch Rendering**:

    o   **Instancing**: If your VR environment contains many repeated objects (like trees or buildings), use **instancing** to render multiple objects with the same mesh in one draw call. This reduces the GPU overhead.

    o   **Batch Rendering**: Combine multiple objects into a single mesh or batch them together to minimize the number of draw calls.

Real-World Example: Optimizing a VR Game to Run Smoothly on Lower-End Hardware

To better understand performance optimization, let's consider a real-world example where we optimize a VR game for smooth performance on lower-end hardware. Let's assume the game is a basic **VR adventure game** where the player explores an expansive environment filled with trees, buildings, and NPCs.

1. **Step 1: Optimizing Assets**:

- Low-Poly Models: All of the trees, buildings, and characters in the environment are created with **low-polygon counts**. The trees, for example, have a simplified trunk and branches, with minimal leaf detail. The buildings are designed with fewer intricate details, and the NPC characters use low-poly bodies and faces.

- Level of Detail (LOD): The game uses multiple LODs for each tree and building. The player won't notice the difference between the high-poly version and the low-poly version when they are far away, but this drastically improves performance.

2. **Step 2: Texture Optimization**:

- Texture Atlases: The game uses a **texture atlas** for all environmental objects. The textures for walls, trees, and props are combined into one large texture sheet, allowing the game to load them more efficiently.

- Compressed Textures: Textures are compressed to reduce memory usage. The resolution of textures for distant objects is reduced, ensuring that they still look decent from afar but don't burden the GPU with unnecessary detail.

3. **Step 3: Efficient Lighting**:

- o **Baked Lighting**: To save on performance, the game uses **baked lighting** for the majority of static objects. The shadows and lighting are precomputed and stored in **lightmaps**, meaning the game doesn't need to perform real-time calculations.
- o **Ambient Occlusion (AO)**: **Ambient occlusion** is baked into the textures, creating subtle shadows around crevices and objects without requiring real-time computation.

4. **Step 4: Use of Simplified Shaders**:
   - o **Simple Materials**: Instead of using complex shaders with reflections, refraction, and transparency, the materials in the game are kept simple. For example, water surfaces are represented with flat textures, and materials like stone or wood have simple color maps with a slight bump effect for added realism.
   - o **Eliminating Expensive Effects**: Effects like **reflections, bloom**, and **motion blur** are either minimized or turned off entirely for lower-end hardware.

5. **Step 5: Testing and Iteration**:
   - o **Playtesting**: After applying optimizations, the game is playtested on various VR hardware, from high-end PCs to low-end systems. The goal is to

ensure that the game runs at a steady **90 FPS** or higher on all systems.

- **Performance Profiling**: Using Unreal's **profiling tools**, such as the **GPU Profiler**, developers can identify any bottlenecks and make adjustments as needed. For example, they might find that NPC AI is too demanding on low-end systems, and would then adjust their behavior or simplify AI logic.

6. **Step 6: Finalizing the Game for Lower-End Hardware**:
   - After optimizations, the game is tested again to ensure it runs smoothly, even on the lowest hardware configurations. Additional tweaks like lowering the resolution of HUD elements or reducing particle effects may be made to enhance performance.

This chapter demonstrated the importance of performance optimization in VR, focusing on high frame rates, reducing polygons, and optimizing textures to maintain a smooth, immersive experience. The real-world example showed how a VR game could be fine-tuned to run well on both high-end and lower-end hardware, ensuring that users across different platforms can enjoy a comfortable and engaging experience. Performance optimization is a crucial skill in VR development and ensures that your game can deliver the best possible experience to as many users as possible.

CHAPTER 10

VR AUDIO: CREATING REALISTIC SOUNDSCAPES

Spatial Audio: How to Integrate 3D Sound into VR Environments

In VR, sound is a critical component for creating a truly immersive experience. Unlike traditional 2D sound, **spatial audio** refers to the ability to hear sounds in three-dimensional space, based on their location relative to the user. This is essential for VR because it helps players to perceive their environment in a more natural and realistic way. Spatial audio is particularly important for immersion, as it mimics the way we hear sounds in the real world.

1. **Understanding Spatial Audio:**
    o   **3D Sound Perception**: In the real world, our brain processes sound based on cues such as the volume, pitch, and time delay between sounds arriving at each ear. This allows us to determine the direction, distance, and movement of sound sources around us.
    o   **Head-Related Transfer Function (HRTF)**: VR audio relies on **HRTF**, a technique used to

simulate how sounds behave in the environment relative to a listener's head. By applying this to the sound, VR systems can simulate how we perceive sound from different directions, which adds a layer of realism and immersion.

2. **Positioning Sounds in 3D Space**:
   o In VR, each sound can be placed in a virtual environment using **positional audio**. This means that the location of a sound source in the game world corresponds to the position where the sound is heard in the virtual environment.
   o For instance, if an object is to the left of the player, the sound emitted from that object will be louder in the left ear than the right, just as it would be in real life. Similarly, the distance from the object affects the volume and quality of the sound.

3. **Doppler Effect**:
   o The **Doppler effect** is another aspect of spatial audio that should be incorporated in dynamic VR environments. As sound sources move relative to the listener (e.g., a passing car or an enemy running), the pitch and frequency of the sound will change. This effect is vital for making VR worlds feel authentic.

4. **Reverb and Echo**:

- o Realistic sound behavior, such as **reverb** (the echo effect that happens when sound bounces off walls or other surfaces), helps create depth in the environment. In VR, reverb should change based on the room's size, materials, and whether the player is inside or outside.

5. **Environment-Based Audio**:
   - o Adjust audio to match the environment. For example, sounds like footsteps on a wooden floor, glass breaking, or birds chirping should feel appropriate to their respective surroundings. A forest should have ambient background sounds, like wind and animals, while an urban setting might feature traffic and distant chatter.

Using Unreal's Audio System: Overview of the Sound Components in Unreal Engine

Unreal Engine provides a comprehensive set of tools for managing audio in your VR projects. From simple sound effects to complex, interactive 3D soundscapes, Unreal Engine's audio system is robust enough to handle the needs of VR development.

1. **Sound Assets**:
   - o Unreal Engine supports various audio file formats, including **WAV**, **MP3**, and **OGG**. You

can import sound assets directly into the **Content Browser**, where they can be assigned to various objects, events, or actions.

2. **Sound Cues**:

   o A **Sound Cue** in Unreal Engine is a system for controlling sound behavior and applying effects, such as mixing, randomizing, or adding reverb. This can be particularly useful for creating complex soundscapes where multiple sounds are layered and played simultaneously.

   o For example, you could create a Sound Cue for footsteps that randomly varies the sound based on different surfaces (e.g., grass, gravel, or wood).

3. **Sound Attenuation**:

   o **Sound Attenuation** refers to the reduction in volume and quality of sound as it moves away from the source. Unreal Engine allows you to control the falloff, the way the sound decreases in volume, and the distance at which it becomes inaudible.

   o You can set up **Attenuation Settings** for any sound actor, which helps simulate realistic sound propagation in VR, such as footsteps fading out as the player moves away from the sound source.

4. **Sound Classes and Groups**:

- o Unreal Engine allows you to organize and control various types of sounds using **Sound Classes** and **Sound Groups**. For instance, you could create a Sound Class for **UI sounds, ambient sounds,** or **combat sounds** and adjust their properties (such as volume, pitch, and effects) globally across your VR environment.

5. **Environmental Audio Effects**:
   - o Unreal's audio system supports **environmental audio effects** such as reverb and occlusion. Reverb can be set to dynamically change based on the player's location in the environment (e.g., echoing footsteps in a hallway or deep reverb in a cave).
   - o You can also control **sound occlusion**, where sounds are muted or muffled based on physical objects blocking the player's view (like a wall or door).

6. **Blueprint Integration**:
   - o Audio events can be triggered and controlled using **Blueprints** in Unreal Engine. For instance, you could create a Blueprint that plays a specific sound when an object is picked up or when a door is opened.

- o Use **Play Sound at Location** or **Play Sound 2D** nodes in Blueprints to trigger sounds based on game events.

7. **Real-Time Dynamic Sound Control**:
   - o In VR, dynamic sound manipulation is often needed. For example, you might want to adjust the volume of background music based on player actions, or have the audio intensity change based on game events like an approaching enemy. Unreal Engine's audio system allows for these dynamic adjustments in real-time, giving developers complete control over the auditory experience.

Real-World Example: Adding Positional Sound to a VR Horror Game

Let's apply these concepts to a real-world example of adding **positional sound** in a VR horror game. In this scenario, the goal is to create a chilling experience where the player feels immersed in an eerie environment, with sounds that heighten tension and suspense.

1. **Setting the Scene**:
   - o Imagine the player is exploring an abandoned mansion at night. The game's goal is to create a

tense atmosphere where sounds seem to come from all directions, enhancing the feeling of fear and unease.

2. **Sound Assets and Ambience**:

   o First, you need to import the right ambient sound assets for the environment. This could include distant thunder, creaking doors, wind howling, and muffled footsteps. These sounds should be subtle but persistent, constantly playing in the background to create a sense of tension.

   o Place **ambient sound cues** for these effects around the mansion's environment, ensuring they are constantly heard but not too loud to be overwhelming. For example, wind sounds could come from outside, while distant footsteps can suggest that the player is not alone.

3. **Positional Audio for Interactive Objects**:

   o As the player moves through the mansion, use **spatial audio** to add positional sound to objects they interact with. For example, if the player opens a door, the sound of the door creaking should come from the direction the player is facing. Similarly, if they walk on different surfaces, such as wood or carpet, their footsteps should produce distinct sounds that react to their movement.

o **Sound Attenuation**: Use sound attenuation to make the footsteps louder when close to the player and fade out as the player moves away, simulating realistic sound propagation.

4. **Dynamic Audio for Horror Elements**:

o Add **dynamic sound cues** triggered by events such as an enemy approaching. For instance, as a monster gets closer, the sound of its breathing, growls, and footsteps will increase in volume and intensity, simulating a real threat.

o **Doppler Effect**: Use the Doppler effect to simulate the sound of the monster moving past the player, making it sound like it's approaching and then receding.

5. **Reverb and Echo Effects**:

o As the player enters different rooms or corridors in the mansion, apply **reverb** to simulate how the environment impacts the sound. For example, in a narrow hallway, footsteps might echo, while in a large, open room, the sound should be more diffused and less pronounced.

6. **Testing and Refining**:

o Test the positional audio and make sure it feels natural. Is the sound direction accurate? Do the footsteps feel realistic when moving around the mansion? Pay close attention to how the audio blends with the visual elements to ensure it amplifies the immersive experience of the game.

o Adjust the volume levels to ensure that the ambient sounds and directional sounds do not compete with each other, creating a balanced and suspenseful environment.

This chapter introduced you to the essential aspects of creating **immersive VR audio**—from **spatial audio** techniques and **sound components** in Unreal Engine to the practical application of positional sound in a **horror game** scenario. Sound in VR is a powerful tool that can significantly enhance the feeling of presence and immersion. By carefully integrating 3D sound, dynamic audio events, and environmental effects, you can create VR experiences that feel as real and engaging as the virtual worlds themselves.

CHAPTER 11

INTERACTIVITY IN VR

User Input: Implementing Button Presses, Gestures, and Voice Commands

User input in VR is a fundamental aspect of creating immersive and interactive experiences. Unlike traditional gaming, where input typically comes from a keyboard, mouse, or controller, VR requires more natural and intuitive methods of interaction. In VR, users often interact with the environment using **motion controllers**, **gestures**, or **voice commands**. Here's how to implement these input methods in your VR projects:

1. **Button Presses**:
   - **Motion Controllers**: Most VR systems use motion controllers that allow players to interact with the virtual world using buttons, triggers, and thumbsticks. The most common buttons used are the **trigger** (to grab or interact), the **grip** (to hold or manipulate objects), and the **thumbstick** (for navigation and selection).
   - **Setting up Button Inputs**:

- In Unreal Engine, button inputs can be configured using **Action Mappings** in the **Project Settings** under **Input**.

- For example, to implement a button press to interact with an object, you would set up a blueprint event that listens for the specific controller button being pressed. When the player presses the button, an action, such as picking up an object or opening a door, would be triggered.

  o **Trigger Actions**: Use the **Trigger** button for interactions that require precise actions, such as grabbing an object or using tools. Unreal Engine allows you to assign actions to the Trigger button using Blueprints.

2. **Gestures**:

  o **Gesture Recognition**: VR systems, such as the Oculus Quest, support hand tracking, which enables users to make **gestures** (such as waving, pointing, or making a fist) to interact with the virtual environment.

  o **Setting up Gesture Input**: Unreal Engine can use **Blueprints** or **C++** to detect gestures. For example, you can detect a **pointing gesture** by tracking the user's hand position and the orientation of their fingers. Once the gesture is recognized, the system can trigger an event, like selecting a button or activating a specific action in the environment.

- **Gesture-Based Interactions**: Many VR applications use hand gestures for actions like opening doors, selecting items from a menu, or signaling enemies. Implementing gesture controls in Unreal requires setting up logic to recognize specific hand movements and trigger the appropriate events.

3. **Voice Commands**:

- **Voice Recognition**: Voice commands in VR allow users to control elements of the experience using natural language. These can be particularly useful in environments where hands-free control is needed, such as in games that require complex interactions or multi-tasking.

- **Implementing Voice Commands in Unreal**: You can integrate voice recognition into your VR project using third-party plugins or middleware like **Google's Speech-to-Text API** or **Microsoft Azure Speech Service**.

  - In Unreal Engine, you would set up a system that listens for specific voice inputs and then triggers corresponding actions. For example, you could say "open the door," and the game would recognize the command and animate the door opening.

- **Voice Feedback**: For voice commands to work effectively, provide **audio feedback** to let users know that their commands have been understood. This could be a simple sound effect or a verbal confirmation like "Command accepted."

Haptic Feedback: Providing Tactile Sensations in VR

Haptic feedback refers to the tactile sensations generated through the controllers, body suits, or even the VR headset, which mimic real-world sensations like touch, force, or texture. In VR, **haptic feedback** plays a vital role in enhancing the immersion by providing players with physical feedback during interactions with the virtual environment.

1. **What is Haptic Feedback?**:
    - **Vibration**: The most common form of haptic feedback is vibration, where the motion controllers vibrate in response to certain events. This can simulate various sensations, like the impact of a bullet hitting a target, the feeling of

an object being thrown, or the sensation of walking on different surfaces.

- o **Force Feedback**: Advanced haptic devices, such as haptic gloves or vests, can simulate force feedback. For instance, if the player is carrying a heavy object, the haptic device could simulate the weight of the object in their hand, creating a more realistic sensation of holding something heavy.

- o **Temperature or Texture Feedback**: Although more complex, some VR systems integrate temperature feedback or tactile sensations that mimic the feeling of different textures, enhancing the realism of the virtual experience.

2. **Integrating Haptic Feedback in Unreal Engine**:
   - o Unreal Engine supports haptic feedback through the **Vibration Component** and various hardware SDKs (e.g., for Oculus and Vive controllers).
   - o **Blueprints for Haptic Feedback**:
     - ▪ Unreal Engine provides **Blueprint** nodes such as **Play Haptic Feedback** to trigger vibrations. You can assign specific vibrations to actions like button presses, picking up objects, or collisions.
     - ▪ For example, when a player picks up an object, you could trigger a vibration on

the motion controller to simulate the weight of the object.

3. **Designing Effective Haptic Feedback**:

   o **Subtlety is Key**: Overusing haptic feedback can overwhelm the player. It's important to design feedback that is subtle but impactful. For example, the sensation of a small vibration when interacting with a button might be more effective than intense vibration when the player is just walking.

   o **Consistency**: Ensure that the haptic feedback is consistent and aligned with the visual and audio cues. For example, if the player hears a door creaking open, the controller should vibrate in a way that matches the sound and motion of the door moving.

Real-World Example: A VR Game Where Haptic Feedback Enhances the Player Experience

Let's explore a practical example of a **VR horror game** where haptic feedback plays a significant role in enhancing the experience. In this example, the player is exploring a haunted mansion, and the game uses haptic feedback to increase the intensity of the atmosphere and interactions.

1. **Scenario Setup**:
   - In the game, players explore a dimly lit mansion. As they move through the dark hallways, they hear eerie sounds like creaking floors, distant whispers, and ghostly groans. The game is designed to immerse players by triggering haptic feedback at key moments.

2. **Haptic Feedback for Interaction**:
   - **Grabbing Objects**: When the player picks up an object (such as an old book or a flashlight), the motion controller vibrates slightly, simulating the weight of the item.
   - **Opening Doors**: As the player opens a door, they feel a subtle rumble in the controllers, mimicking the physical sensation of pushing the door open. The feedback is more intense when the door is heavy or difficult to move.
   - **Ghostly Encounters**: When a ghostly figure suddenly appears behind the player, the controllers deliver a sharp vibration, simulating a sudden scare or shock. This could be coupled with a louder audio cue for added immersion.

3. **Using Haptics to Simulate Horror Elements**:
   - **Heartbeat Simulation**: As the player's stress levels increase (due to encountering enemies or exploring dangerous areas), the controller

vibrates in rhythm with the player's **heartbeat**, simulating a racing pulse and heightening the feeling of tension.

o **Environmental Feedback**: The player encounters different floors in the mansion: creaky wood floors give a different haptic response than carpeted areas. When stepping on a hard surface, the controllers deliver a sharp, quick vibration. When walking on soft ground, the vibration is more subdued and slow.

4. **Enhancing Fear with Unexpected Haptics**:

o At key moments, such as when the player is looking at a creepy painting or walking past an abandoned mirror, the game triggers a sudden burst of haptic feedback, simulating the feeling of something brushing against the player's hands or back, even though nothing is physically present.

o This unexpected sensation enhances the horror experience and helps to build an atmosphere of uncertainty and fear, making players feel as though they are truly in the haunted mansion.

This chapter covered how to implement user input through **button presses, gestures**, and **voice commands**, as well as how to integrate **haptic feedback** to enhance immersion in VR. By using these techniques, you can create more interactive and tactile experiences that fully engage the player. The real-world example of the **VR horror game** showed how haptic feedback can play a key role in intensifying the player's emotional response, making the virtual world feel more real and responsive. By thoughtfully incorporating these elements into your VR projects, you can design more intuitive and immersive environments that captivate your audience.

CHAPTER 12

CREATING REALISTIC PHYSICS FOR VR

Unreal Physics Engine: Using Unreal's Physics for Interactive VR Environments

The physics engine in Unreal Engine is a powerful tool for creating dynamic and realistic interactions in VR. Realistic physics adds to the immersion by allowing objects to move, interact, and respond to player actions in a believable way. Unreal Engine's physics system is highly customizable, supporting everything from basic object interactions to complex simulations like fluid dynamics and rigid body simulations.

1. **Overview of Unreal's Physics Engine**:
    o Unreal Engine uses a built-in physics engine known as **Chaos Physics**, which handles the real-time simulation of physical behaviors like gravity, collisions, and object movement.
    o The engine supports two main types of physical simulation:
        ▪ **Rigid Body Dynamics (RBD)**: This simulates the motion of solid objects

under forces, including gravity, friction, and collisions.

- **Soft Body Physics**: For deformable objects, Unreal's Chaos Physics can also simulate soft-body behaviors (like squishy objects), although this is more complex and typically used in specialized scenarios.

2. **Using Physics in VR**:

   o Physics-driven interactions in VR are vital to creating immersive experiences. VR environments must simulate realistic object behaviors, like throwing, dropping, or bouncing objects, based on their physical properties.

   o In Unreal Engine, you can enable physics for an object by turning on its **Simulate Physics** property in the **Details Panel**. This will allow the object to respond to forces, gravity, and collisions.

3. **Applying Forces**:

   o **Forces** in Unreal Engine can be applied to objects dynamically. For example, you can apply a force when a player throws an object or when they push against a wall.

- **Impulse**: This is an instantaneous force that changes the velocity of an object (e.g., a sudden push or kick).
- **Continuous Force**: Forces like gravity or wind can continuously affect an object's movement.

4. **Physics Materials**:
   - In VR, the interaction of objects depends on their physical properties, such as **friction, bounciness**, and **density**. These can be set using **Physics Materials** in Unreal Engine.
     - For example, you might assign a **bouncy** physics material to a rubber ball so that it behaves realistically when thrown or dropped, or a **slippery** material to ice so objects slide around easily.

5. **Realistic Interactions**:
   - In VR, the player should feel a realistic response when interacting with physical objects. For example, when the player grabs a heavy object, the VR system should account for the object's mass and make the motion feel as though it requires effort.

Collision Detection: Handling Objects Colliding in VR

In VR, handling **collisions**—when objects bump into or interact with each other—plays a vital role in creating immersive and interactive environments. Accurate collision detection ensures that objects in the VR world behave as they would in real life.

1. **What is Collision Detection?**
    o   **Collision detection** refers to the process of detecting when two or more objects in the game world touch or intersect. It's essential in VR for simulating interactions, such as a player picking up an object, a projectile hitting a target, or objects colliding with walls.
    o   Unreal Engine offers various types of collision detection systems, including **simple collision** (bounding boxes, spheres) and **complex collision** (mesh-based detection for more detailed interactions).

2. **Types of Collision in Unreal Engine**:
    o   **Simple Collision**: Simple collision shapes, like spheres, boxes, and capsules, are used for basic interactions. These shapes are easier to compute and are less taxing on performance. For instance, a **sphere** is used for a ball, or a **box** for a crate.
    o   **Complex Collision**: More accurate and detailed collisions are possible using the **mesh** of the

object itself, though these are more computationally expensive. Complex collisions are necessary for objects with intricate or irregular shapes, such as character models or uneven terrain.

3. **Collision Channels and Responses**:

   o Unreal Engine allows you to define **collision channels** and **response types** for different objects. For example, you can specify that a character can walk through a door but collide with walls. You can customize how objects interact by choosing from options like **Block**, **Overlap**, or **Ignore**.

   o Collision responses in VR should feel natural. For example, when a player grabs an object, it should "snap" to the player's hand. When the player's hand collides with a solid object (like a wall or another character), the VR interaction should stop, and the player's hand should bounce off slightly.

4. **Physics and Collision for Interactivity**:

   o Combining **physics** and **collision detection** allows for rich, interactive experiences. For example, if a player pushes an object, the object should move based on the collision response and react to external forces like friction or gravity.

- o Unreal Engine's **Physics Constraints** can be used to simulate objects that are constrained in some way, such as doors that open or hinges that allow limited movement.

5. **Optimizing Collision in VR**:
    - o To maintain a smooth experience in VR, avoid overly complex collision calculations in real-time. For instance, large, complex meshes should use simplified collision models for better performance. You can optimize by using **custom collision boxes** or **convex meshes** for large objects instead of using the full object geometry.

Real-World Example: A VR Simulation of a Physics-Based Puzzle Game

Let's walk through how to create a **VR physics-based puzzle game**, where players solve puzzles by manipulating objects in the environment. In this example, we will focus on optimizing the physics and collision detection to create a realistic, interactive experience.

1. **Scenario Setup**:
    - o The player is inside a virtual room with a series of physics-based puzzles. The goal is to move a series of weighted objects, stack them in a certain

order, and use them to trigger mechanisms (such as opening a door or lifting a platform).

2. **Step 1: Create Physics Objects**:
   - First, create basic objects like **crates**, **weights**, and **buttons**. In Unreal Engine, enable **Simulate Physics** for these objects to allow them to react to forces like gravity.
   - For each object, assign an appropriate **physics material**. For example, crates might have **low friction**, while weights should be **dense** and difficult to move.

3. **Step 2: Collision Setup**:
   - For each object, define its **collision** properties. Crates might have a **simple box collision**, while the button could use a **complex mesh collision**.
   - Set up **collision responses** so that when the player throws a crate at the button, it triggers a mechanism, like a lever pulling down or a door opening. The collision should feel natural, so the button should "push" down when the crate lands on it, simulating a real-world interaction.

4. **Step 3: Creating the Puzzle Mechanics**:
   - The player needs to stack a series of objects in the correct order to solve the puzzle. Use Unreal's **Blueprint system** to create an interactive system where the player can grab and stack objects.

- o Apply **force or torque** to simulate the weight and inertia of the objects when the player moves them. If a player pushes a heavy object, it should require more force to move.

5. **Step 4: Implementing Feedback and Interaction**:
   - o **Haptic Feedback**: As the player moves objects, trigger subtle **haptic feedback** to simulate the weight and friction of the objects. When the player grabs a crate, the controller could vibrate based on the weight, giving the player a sense of the object's mass.
   - o **Physics-Based Reactions**: When the player moves or drops objects, they should interact with each other realistically. If the player knocks over a stack of boxes, the objects should topple and fall based on their weight, creating a satisfying physics-based reaction.

6. **Step 5: Testing and Refining the Gameplay**:
   - o Playtest the game in VR to ensure that interactions feel smooth and realistic. Check for any issues with the collision detection (e.g., objects not behaving as expected when colliding or intersecting) and optimize physics settings to maintain a stable frame rate.
   - o Fine-tune the physics and collision responses. For example, adjust the **mass** and **friction** of objects

to make the puzzles more challenging or easier, depending on the player's desired difficulty level.

This chapter provided an overview of creating realistic physics in VR environments, including how to use **Unreal Engine's physics engine**, set up **collision detection**, and optimize interactive elements for immersive VR experiences. The real-world example of a **physics-based puzzle game** demonstrated how these concepts come together to create a dynamic, engaging, and interactive VR world where objects respond realistically to player actions. By integrating these physics techniques, you can build highly interactive and immersive environments that enhance gameplay and user experience.

CHAPTER 13

DESIGNING USER INTERFACES (UI) FOR VR

Challenges of VR UI: Designing Intuitive, Non-Intrusive UIs

Designing user interfaces (UI) for Virtual Reality (VR) presents a unique set of challenges compared to traditional desktop or mobile design. In VR, the user is immersed in a three-dimensional space, so the UI needs to feel as natural and intuitive as possible without breaking the immersive experience. The goal is to design UIs that are functional, easily navigable, and integrated seamlessly into the virtual environment.

1. **Intuition and Ease of Use**:
   - o Traditional UIs (e.g., mouse-and-keyboard or touchscreen) rely on flat, 2D screens where users can quickly understand where to click, tap, or hover. In VR, however, the interface exists in 3D space, and the user interacts through hand movements, gestures, or controllers.
   - o The challenge is ensuring that the interface is **intuitive**. Users must be able to interact with elements without needing to memorize

complicated control schemes. For instance, buttons should be large enough to be selected easily, and menus should be placed within the player's natural field of view.

2. **Non-Intrusiveness**:
   o One of the primary goals of VR UI design is to ensure that the UI doesn't break the immersion. If the UI is overly intrusive or cluttered, it can detract from the experience and cause discomfort or distraction.

   o **Minimalist Design**: To maintain immersion, VR UIs should be as unobtrusive as possible. This means using a minimalist approach to elements like menus, buttons, and overlays, which should appear only when necessary and fade out when not in use.

   o **Spatial Placement**: Placing UI elements in a spatially appropriate way is also essential. For instance, menus should be positioned so that they feel like part of the environment and don't block the user's view of the scene. The interface can be set to appear in the user's periphery or be activated when the user looks at a specific area.

3. **Contextual Awareness**:
   o In VR, the UI must be **context-sensitive**. For example, interactive elements should appear only

when needed, like when the user is close to an object or when an action is possible (e.g., a button appears when the user reaches for a door).

o The UI should also adapt dynamically to the user's actions or location in the VR environment. For instance, when a player grabs an object, a UI element might appear in their hand, providing more information or options related to that object.

4. **Depth and Scale**:

o **3D vs. 2D UI**: Unlike traditional 2D interfaces, VR interfaces exist in a 3D space. Elements like buttons, sliders, and menus need to be designed with appropriate depth and scale, allowing users to interact with them naturally.

o **UI Distance**: The user must be able to comfortably reach and interact with UI elements in 3D space. Too close, and it may feel overwhelming; too far, and it becomes difficult to interact with. UI should be placed within a **comfortable reach** or be easily accessible with gestures or controllers.

VR Widgets and Menus: Creating 3D UIs and Holographic Interfaces

VR enables the creation of **3D UI elements** and **holographic interfaces** that go beyond traditional 2D screens, offering new ways for users to interact with their environment. Here's how to leverage Unreal Engine's tools to create immersive, interactive VR widgets and menus:

1. **Creating 3D Widgets**:
    o   In VR, **3D widgets** are the equivalent of traditional UI elements, such as buttons, sliders, or text fields, but they exist as objects in the virtual world. These can be placed in the environment for the user to interact with using their hands or controllers.
    o   Unreal Engine's **Widget Blueprint** system allows developers to create 3D UI elements that can be manipulated within the VR space. You can use the **UUserWidget** class to create interactive elements that behave like traditional widgets but exist in 3D space.
    o   **3D Buttons and Sliders**: Buttons in VR can be created as physical objects that users can reach out and press or grab. Similarly, sliders can be used for adjusting variables such as volume or

brightness, using a hand movement to slide the object along a track.

2. **Holographic Menus**:

   o **Holographic UIs** in VR can be designed to resemble floating menus, icons, or dashboards that are fully interactive. These interfaces can be projected as if they are floating in the user's virtual world, giving the illusion of interacting with a futuristic or sci-fi environment.

   o To create **holographic menus**, you can use **Widget Components** in Unreal Engine. These components can display 3D widgets in the virtual world that are anchored to a particular spot or move as the player's viewpoint shifts.

   o **Interactive Holographic Buttons**: You can design menus that appear when the user triggers a specific action, such as looking at an object, and disappear when they stop interacting. The holographic buttons could have glowing effects or animations to give them a high-tech appearance.

3. **World-Space UI**:

   o **World-space widgets** are 3D objects within the environment that function as UI elements. For example, a floating HUD (heads-up display) showing the player's health, inventory, or mission objectives could be anchored in the world-space.

o   World-space UI is ideal for VR environments because it integrates naturally into the virtual world. As the player moves, the UI moves with them, which keeps it in their line of sight without obstructing the world itself.

o   The key here is to ensure that world-space UI is placed in an intuitive location, such as in the player's field of view but not too close to the camera, to avoid distracting them from the virtual environment.

4. **Interaction with 3D UIs**:

o   **Grabbing and Clicking**: In VR, a common method of interacting with 3D UIs is using a hand controller's **trigger** or **grip** buttons to grab, click, or manipulate UI elements. You can assign interactions like grabbing and rotating to specific actions, like turning a knob or pressing a button.

o   **Gesture-Based Interactions**: In addition to button presses, **gestures** can also be used for UI interaction. For example, the player could wave their hand to scroll through a menu, point at a button to select it, or make a pinch gesture to zoom in on an object.

Real-World Example: VR UI Design in a Virtual Desktop Environment

Let's consider a **VR desktop environment** where the user can interact with virtual screens, windows, and controls using hand gestures and controllers. This type of environment is a perfect example of how to implement 3D widgets, holographic UIs, and interactive menus to create a fully immersive and intuitive VR interface.

1. **Scenario Setup**:
   - o In the VR desktop environment, the player puts on a VR headset and enters a virtual office space. The space is filled with floating windows and interactive elements like desktop icons, documents, and virtual keyboards. The user can interact with these elements using their VR controllers or hand gestures.

2. **Step 1: Creating Virtual Screens and Windows**:
   - o **Virtual Monitors**: To start, we create several **virtual monitors** in the 3D space. These can be **3D widgets** anchored in front of the user's view. On these virtual screens, the player can open applications, browse the internet, or view media.
   - o **Holographic UI**: The windows on the virtual desktop are holographic, giving the illusion of floating screens in front of the user. The user can

drag these windows around, resize them, or open new ones using their controllers or hand gestures.

3. **Step 2: Creating Interactive Menus**:

   o **Toolbar and Icons**: The desktop contains a toolbar with icons for different applications (e.g., a web browser, file explorer, or settings). These icons are interactive 3D buttons. When the user looks at them and presses the button on the controller, the respective application opens.

   o **Hover and Click Effects**: To make the interaction more immersive, hovering the controller pointer over an icon can cause the icon to glow or animate, indicating that it is interactable. Clicking the button opens the application, and the window appears as a floating UI element.

4. **Step 3: Interaction with Documents and Files**:

   o **Grabbing Documents**: When the player needs to interact with a document or file, the player can reach out and **grab** it. Once grabbed, the player can move it around, rotate it, or open it by interacting with it.

   o **Scrolling**: The player can scroll through documents by using their thumbstick or a gesture, such as swiping the air or using a virtual scroll wheel.

5. **Step 4: Additional Interaction Elements**:

   o **Virtual Keyboard**: A virtual keyboard can be added to the desktop environment. The user can click on the keys using hand gestures or controllers. The keys could be holographic and appear as a floating object in front of the player, maintaining the illusion of a physical keyboard.

6. **Step 5: Testing and Refining the UI**:

   o Test the interaction flow in **VR Preview** mode to ensure the interface feels natural and intuitive. The desktop environment should feel functional but also immersive, with no unnecessary interruptions or overly complex controls.

   o Adjust the placement of UI elements so they remain within the user's field of view but are not too close, ensuring that they can interact with them without strain.

This chapter explored the unique challenges of designing **user interfaces (UIs)** for VR, from creating **intuitive, non-intrusive designs** to implementing **3D widgets** and **holographic interfaces**. By examining a **virtual desktop environment** as a real-world example, we demonstrated how to build immersive, functional, and intuitive VR UIs that enhance the user experience. With the right balance of interactive elements, clear navigation, and spatial placement, VR UIs can become as natural and engaging as interacting with the physical world.

CHAPTER 14

AI FOR VIRTUAL REALITY

Integrating AI in VR: Using Unreal's AI System for NPC Behaviors in VR

Artificial Intelligence (AI) is an essential component in many VR experiences, especially when it comes to creating dynamic, responsive NPCs (Non-Playable Characters). AI can help drive the behavior and decision-making of characters, making them feel more alive and reactive to the player's actions, which enhances the immersion and overall experience.

1. **Unreal Engine's AI System**:
   - Unreal Engine has a comprehensive AI system designed to manage NPCs and environmental interactions. This includes **behavior trees**, **blackboards**, and **nav meshes**, which allow AI-controlled characters to navigate and react intelligently within a VR environment.
   - **Behavior Trees**: A behavior tree is a decision tree used to define the logic for NPC actions. For example, an NPC might have a behavior tree that directs it to patrol an area, chase a player, or take

cover. This system allows for complex, hierarchical decision-making processes that are necessary for realistic NPC behavior in VR.

- o **Blackboards**: Blackboards store variables and states that the behavior tree can use. For example, the blackboard could store the position of the player or an NPC's health status, influencing decisions made by the behavior tree.

- o **Nav Meshes**: Nav meshes are used to define walkable areas in the game world. They enable NPCs to navigate the environment intelligently, avoiding obstacles and moving towards specific targets. For VR, it's crucial that NPCs move fluidly and realistically, adjusting their pathfinding as needed based on the player's position.

2. **Setting Up AI for VR**:
   - o To get started, you can use Unreal Engine's **AI Controller** class, which is responsible for controlling the AI's behavior. The AI controller can be assigned to an NPC, allowing it to make decisions based on the environment and the player's actions.
   - o For instance, if the player enters a certain area, the NPC might notice them and begin to follow them. This could be triggered by the **sight**

perception system in Unreal, which uses the NPC's field of view and line-of-sight calculations to detect the player.

- o You can also integrate **sound detection** using the AI perception system. For example, if the player makes noise (like walking through water or knocking over an object), the NPC could hear the sound and investigate its source.

3. **AI Perception in VR:**

- o AI perception in VR is vital for creating realistic and engaging NPC behaviors. Using Unreal's **AI Perception System**, NPCs can detect stimuli like sight, sound, and smell. The **Sight** and **Hearing** systems can be used to detect when the player moves into an NPC's line of sight or makes a noise.

- o This can be customized to include things like how far an NPC can "see," how well they can detect the player based on lighting conditions, or how sensitive they are to sound. These factors contribute to creating more immersive and interactive NPC behaviors that respond naturally to player actions.

Creating Interactive NPCs: Using AI to Respond to User Actions

NPCs are a core component of many VR experiences, and using AI to create responsive, interactive NPCs can drastically enhance the immersion and engagement in a VR world. Creating NPCs that react to user actions can be done in various ways, from simple interactions (like greetings) to complex reactions (like combat or conversations).

1. **Setting Up AI-Driven NPC Interactions**:
   - **Reacting to the Player**: The simplest form of AI interaction involves making NPCs react when the player approaches or performs a specific action. For instance, an NPC may stop what they're doing and look at the player when the player walks near them. This can be achieved by configuring the **AI perception system** to trigger events when the player enters an NPC's detection range.
   - **Conversational AI**: To make NPCs more interactive, you can implement basic conversational systems where NPCs respond to the player's input. This can be done using **dialogue trees** or even more sophisticated AI systems that generate responses dynamically. The AI can recognize specific keywords or voice commands and respond appropriately.

135

- **Dynamic Responses Based on Player Actions**: More complex interactions can be achieved by having NPCs respond to the player's actions in real-time. For example, if the player behaves aggressively towards an NPC, the NPC could flee, become hostile, or call for help. Conversely, if the player helps an NPC or performs a positive action, the NPC might thank the player, offer assistance, or reward them.

2. **Emotion and Behavior Systems**:

- NPCs in VR can be programmed to exhibit emotions based on the player's actions. For example, NPCs can become fearful when the player draws a weapon, or they can express happiness when the player offers them something. This adds another layer of realism, as the NPCs are not just mindlessly following commands but reacting to the player as a living entity would.

- **NPC Behavior States**: You can set up different behavioral states for NPCs that change based on certain conditions, such as:
  - **Idle**: When the NPC is resting or standing still.
  - **Alert**: When the NPC is on guard, paying attention to potential threats.

- **Aggressive**: When the NPC decides to fight back against the player.
- **Fleeing**: When the NPC runs away to avoid danger.

3. **Non-Verbal Interactions**:

   o In VR, it's important that NPCs don't just talk—they should also communicate through body language and non-verbal cues. You can animate NPCs to look towards the player when they're being addressed, or perform actions like shaking their head in disapproval or nodding when agreeing with the player.

   o Unreal's **Animation Blueprint** system allows you to control how NPCs move, express themselves, and respond to the player's actions, making them feel more lifelike and interactive.

Real-World Example: AI-Driven Characters in a VR Game

Let's look at an example of implementing **AI-driven characters** in a VR game. Consider a **VR survival game** where the player is trapped in a dangerous wilderness, interacting with NPCs for supplies, guidance, and survival tips.

1. **Scenario Setup**:

o The player encounters an NPC, a fellow survivor, who offers guidance on how to build shelter and find food. As the player interacts with the NPC, the NPC's behavior and dialogue change based on the player's actions and decisions.

2. **Step 1: Implementing AI Perception for NPC Awareness**:

   o The first step is setting up the **AI perception system** for the NPC. The NPC is set to detect the player's position using the **sight and sound** perception components.

   o If the player moves too quickly or aggressively, the NPC might become wary, adjusting its behavior to reflect this change.

   o Conversely, if the player approaches the NPC calmly or offers assistance, the NPC's perception state could switch to friendly, and it might offer help.

3. **Step 2: Dynamic Reactions to Player Actions**:

   o **Combat and Aggression**: If the player pulls out a weapon, the NPC can become fearful and attempt to flee, or they might become hostile and prepare to defend themselves. These behaviors are triggered by the player's **AI perception** system detecting the weapon or aggressive movement.

- o **Help or Betrayal**: If the player helps the NPC, the NPC could reward them with useful items, such as food, water, or shelter-building materials. On the other hand, if the player betrays the NPC (perhaps by stealing their supplies), the NPC could react negatively, potentially becoming hostile or warning other NPCs.

4. **Step 3: Emotional and Behavioral States**:

- o As the player interacts with the NPC, their **emotion state** changes. For example, if the player shows kindness or provides food, the NPC's behavior state could change from "Neutral" to "Grateful" and they might express emotions like happiness or relief.

- o If the player chooses to be hostile or steals, the NPC's state might change to "Angry" or "Suspicious," leading to different dialogue and behavior patterns.

5. **Step 4: Non-Verbal Communication and Immersion**:

- o Non-verbal communication plays a big role in VR. The NPC could use gestures or body language, such as raising their hands in fear if the player approaches too quickly, or shaking their head when asked a question that they can't answer.

o   This helps make the NPC feel more realistic and interactive, contributing to the immersive nature of VR.

6.   **Step 5: Testing and Refining AI Interactions**:

o   Playtesting is critical to ensure the NPC behaviors feel natural and responsive. You need to ensure the AI reacts to the player in a way that feels consistent with the game world. Testing can also help fine-tune the difficulty level of the interactions (e.g., ensuring NPCs aren't too aggressive or too passive).

This chapter explored how to integrate AI into VR environments using Unreal Engine's powerful AI system. We discussed setting up **NPC behaviors** with **AI perception**, creating **interactive NPCs** that respond to user actions, and implementing dynamic emotional and behavioral states. The real-world example of **AI-driven characters** in a **VR survival game** demonstrated how to create immersive and interactive NPCs that adapt and react to player choices. With AI, you can bring virtual worlds to life, creating engaging and responsive environments that enhance the player's experience.

CHAPTER 15

VR NETWORKING AND MULTIPLAYER

Basics of Networking in VR: Implementing Multiplayer and Networking Features

In Virtual Reality (VR), networking and multiplayer functionality are essential for creating shared experiences where multiple players can interact within the same virtual world. The challenge with VR multiplayer is not only ensuring that players can see and interact with each other but also maintaining smooth performance, synchronization, and a high level of immersion across different VR systems.

1. **Multiplayer Concepts in VR**:
    o **Client-Server Architecture**: Most VR multiplayer games use a **client-server** model. In this model, one player (the host) acts as the server, while the other players (clients) connect to the server to exchange data. The server is responsible for managing the game world, handling game logic, and keeping the game state synchronized for all players.

- o **Peer-to-Peer Networking**: While client-server is the most common model, some games may use **peer-to-peer (P2P)** networking. This allows all players to communicate directly with each other without the need for a central server. However, P2P models are more complex in terms of synchronization and can lead to issues like lag and inconsistencies.

- o **Latency and Bandwidth**: VR multiplayer requires low latency and high bandwidth to maintain a seamless experience. High latency (delays in data transmission) can cause lag, making interactions jerky or out of sync, which is especially critical in VR where precise timing and smooth motion are vital for immersion.

2. **Data Synchronization in VR**:

- o **State Synchronization**: Ensuring that the game state is synchronized across all players is crucial. This means that when one player interacts with an object, other players should see that object react in real-time. Unreal Engine provides several methods for synchronization, such as **replication** and **networked actors**, which allow game state to be shared across multiple clients.

- o **Replication**: In Unreal Engine, **replication** is the process of sending an object's state (like position, rotation, or health) from the server to the clients. This ensures that every player in the game sees the same thing and that changes in the game world are reflected consistently across all players.

- o **Prediction and Interpolation**: To handle lag, games often use prediction and interpolation techniques. **Prediction** involves anticipating where an object will be based on its current velocity and updating its position accordingly. **Interpolation** smooths out movement between data updates, reducing the perception of lag.

Server and Client Communication: How Data is Exchanged Between VR Players

In multiplayer VR games, the communication between the server and client is central to ensuring all players experience the same game world. Unreal Engine's networking system makes it easy to implement and manage this data exchange.

1. **How Server-Client Communication Works**:
   - o **Server's Role**: The server manages the authoritative game state, including player positions, object interactions, and game logic. It is responsible for keeping track of the world and ensuring consistency for all players.

- o **Client's Role**: Each client only controls the local player's actions (movement, gestures, etc.) and sends these inputs to the server. The client receives updates from the server about other players, objects, and events in the game world.

2. **Replicating Data**:
   - o Unreal Engine uses **network replication** to ensure data is sent from the server to clients. This includes the position and rotation of actors (such as players and objects), animation states, and player actions.
     - **Replicated Variables**: You can set specific variables to be replicated from the server to all connected clients. For example, when a player picks up an object, the position of that object will be replicated to all other clients.
     - **RPCs (Remote Procedure Calls)**: RPCs are used to send specific functions from the server to clients or from clients to the server. This could be used to trigger actions like opening a door or starting an animation on another player's character.

3. **Latency Compensation**:
   - o In multiplayer VR, latency is an important factor. Delays can disrupt the experience, causing

144

objects to lag behind the player's movements. **Lag compensation** techniques are used to predict and smooth out the impact of latency.

- **Client-Side Prediction**: Clients predict the movement of objects (such as other players) and adjust their display until the server's true position is received.
- **Server Reconciliation**: The server periodically sends corrections to the client to reconcile predicted positions with the actual positions. This helps to reduce discrepancies caused by latency.

4. **Handling User Input**:
   o **Client Input**: Each player sends their input (e.g., hand movements, gestures, controller actions) to the server, which then updates the game state and broadcasts it to all connected clients.
   o **Server Validation**: The server validates the input it receives to ensure that actions are legitimate (e.g., checking whether a player can open a door or pick up an item based on the current game state).

5. **Voice Chat and Communication**:
   o Many multiplayer VR games include **voice chat** to allow players to communicate. This data is typically handled via a voice server, which

transmits the player's audio to all clients in real-time. Unreal Engine supports voice chat integration via the **Online Subsystem** and **Voice Chat Component**, which enables voice communication between players in a networked environment.

Real-World Example: A Multiplayer VR Game (e.g., "Rec Room")
for Hands-on Understanding

To better understand VR networking and multiplayer, let's look at a real-world example: **"Rec Room"**, a popular multiplayer VR game that allows players to meet up in virtual rooms to engage in games and socialize. Here's how multiplayer features are implemented in such a VR game.

1. **Scenario Setup**:
   - In "Rec Room," players join virtual rooms where they can interact with other players, play games, and explore the environment. The multiplayer experience allows users to engage in activities together, such as playing laser tag, building objects, or chatting with friends in a virtual social space.
2. **Step 1: Multiplayer Setup**:

- o **Joining a Room**: When a player enters the game, they connect to a **central server** (hosted on the cloud or by a player), which acts as the authoritative source of the game world. The player's avatar, along with any objects they interact with, are replicated to all other players in the same room.

- o **Data Replication**: As players move and interact with objects, their positions, actions, and states (e.g., health, inventory) are replicated to all clients. This ensures that everyone in the room sees the same thing.

3. **Step 2: Server and Client Communication**:

- o **Host and Clients**: In "Rec Room," the game uses a **hosted peer-to-peer** model. One player's machine becomes the host, and other players connect to it as clients. The host manages game logic and state synchronization.

- o **Input Handling**: Each client sends input to the host (e.g., moving the avatar, pressing buttons) via the network. The host processes this input and updates the game world, then replicates these updates to all other clients.

4. **Step 3: Voice Chat and Social Interaction**:

- o **Real-Time Voice Chat**: Players can use voice chat to communicate while playing. "Rec Room" uses spatialized voice chat, meaning players can hear others based on their location in the virtual environment. For instance, if two players are far apart in the virtual world, their voices will sound quieter, and if they move closer, their voices will become clearer.

- o **Synchronization**: Voice data is transmitted in real-time via the server, ensuring that all players hear their friends' voices with low latency, improving the feeling of presence and interaction.

5. **Step 4: Minimizing Latency and Improving Sync**:
   - o **Prediction and Interpolation**: To handle network latency, "Rec Room" uses client-side prediction to ensure that movement feels smooth and responsive. Even if there's a slight delay in data transmission, the game can predict player movements to reduce the perception of lag.
   - o **Syncing Player Actions**: The game uses regular updates to synchronize actions between players. For example, when one player picks up an object or moves a virtual item, all other players see the action happen almost simultaneously, thanks to replicated data and updates.

6. **Step 5: Testing and Optimizing Multiplayer Features**:
   - o During development, extensive testing is conducted to ensure smooth multiplayer

performance. This involves simulating various network conditions (such as high latency or packet loss) and adjusting settings to ensure the game remains playable under all circumstances.

o **Optimizing Bandwidth**: "Rec Room" optimizes bandwidth usage by only sending necessary data (like player positions, actions, and voice chat) to minimize latency and reduce the amount of data that needs to be transferred.

This chapter provided an in-depth look at **VR networking and multiplayer** functionality in Unreal Engine. We covered how to implement **server-client communication**, **replication**, and **latency compensation** to ensure smooth and synchronized gameplay. The **real-world example of "Rec Room"** demonstrated how multiplayer VR experiences are structured and optimized, giving a hands-on understanding of how multiplayer features work in a VR environment. By integrating networking principles into your VR projects, you can create engaging multiplayer experiences that allow players to interact seamlessly in the virtual world.

CHAPTER 16

BUILDING FOR DIFFERENT VR PLATFORMS

PC VR vs. Standalone VR: Differences and Optimization Tips

Virtual Reality (VR) platforms are diverse, with two major categories: **PC VR** and **Standalone VR**. These platforms differ in terms of performance capabilities, hardware requirements, and user experiences. Understanding these differences is crucial for optimizing VR experiences across various devices.

1. **PC VR**:

    o **Hardware Requirements**: PC VR systems, such as the **HTC Vive**, **Oculus Rift**, and **Valve Index**, rely on high-performance computers to run VR experiences. These systems are typically connected to a PC via cables and require a **high-end GPU** and **processor** to render detailed environments smoothly.

    o **Performance**: PC VR offers higher graphical fidelity because it leverages the power of the host computer. This allows developers to create more complex and detailed virtual environments with higher frame rates and more demanding effects (e.g., real-time lighting, complex physics simulations).

- o **Optimization Tips**:
  - **Higher Graphics Settings**: Since PC VR has access to powerful hardware, developers can afford to push the boundaries of graphical quality. Make sure to take full advantage of **advanced shaders**, **lighting effects**, and **realistic physics**.
  - **Use LOD (Level of Detail)**: Implement **LOD techniques** to optimize performance without sacrificing visual fidelity. LOD adjusts the complexity of objects based on their distance from the player, reducing polygon count and texture size for objects further away.
  - **Performance Profiling**: Regularly use Unreal Engine's **GPU profiler** to ensure that the game runs smoothly at **90 FPS** or higher.

2. **Standalone VR**:
   - o **Hardware Requirements**: Standalone VR headsets like the **Oculus Quest 2** are self-contained units with built-in processing, storage,

and display. They don't need a connection to a PC, which makes them portable and more accessible. However, the hardware (CPU, GPU, RAM) is more limited compared to PC VR systems.

o **Performance**: Standalone VR offers a more portable experience but with some trade-offs in graphical fidelity. The lower processing power means that graphics must be optimized for smooth performance without overloading the system.

o **Optimization Tips**:

- **Lower-Resolution Assets**: Use **lower-resolution textures** and **simplified models** to reduce the processing load. Ensure that assets are optimized for mobile GPUs.

- **Baked Lighting and Shadows**: Since real-time lighting can be performance-heavy, use **baked lighting** for static objects to improve performance while keeping the visuals appealing.

- **Efficient Meshes**: Keep the polygon count low and avoid complex geometries. Use **mesh simplification** and **LOD** techniques to ensure smooth performance, especially for larger environments.

- **Optimize Frame Rate**: Since the Oculus Quest runs at **72 FPS** or **90 FPS**, optimize your game to meet these frame rate targets while maintaining comfort for the user.

Cross-Platform VR Development: Creating Experiences for Multiple VR Headsets

As the VR market expands, developing experiences that work across a wide range of devices becomes increasingly important. **Cross-platform VR development** allows developers to create applications that are compatible with both PC VR and standalone headsets like the **Oculus Quest**.

1. **Challenges of Cross-Platform Development**:
    - **Hardware and Performance Differences**: The most significant challenge is ensuring that the game runs smoothly across platforms with different processing power, memory, and input methods.
    - **Control and Interaction Variability**: Different VR headsets come with varying controllers and input methods. For example, the Oculus Quest 2

uses **hand tracking** and **Oculus Touch controllers**, while the HTC Vive uses **Vive controllers** and has **external sensors** for room tracking.

o **Field of View and Display Differences**: The field of view (FOV), resolution, and refresh rate can vary between devices, requiring adjustments to ensure consistency across platforms.

2. **Best Practices for Cross-Platform VR Development**:

o **Abstract Input Systems**: Use Unreal Engine's **Input Mapping** system to abstract the input methods, allowing your game to handle different controllers and input devices seamlessly. Define a **unified input model** that maps gestures, buttons, and motion actions across platforms.

▪ For instance, both Oculus and Vive controllers can be mapped to the same in-game actions, such as **grabbing an object** or **triggering a menu**, even though their physical buttons may differ.

o **Quality Settings and Graphics Scalability**: To ensure that your game looks good and runs smoothly across both high-end and low-end platforms, use **dynamic quality settings**. This allows you to adjust the resolution, texture quality, and effects depending on the platform's performance capabilities.

- For example, on a **PC VR** headset, you can use **higher resolution textures** and **advanced shaders**, while on a **standalone VR headset**, you can reduce these features to maintain frame rate stability.

o **Consistent UX/UI Design**: When designing the **user interface** (UI), ensure that elements like menus, buttons, and icons are scalable and adaptable to different screen sizes and resolutions. For example, a floating menu might work on both platforms, but the size and positioning of elements should adjust based on the device's screen and resolution.

o **Networking and Multiplayer Considerations**: In multiplayer VR games, ensure that the networking code is designed to handle communication between players using different headsets. Keep in mind that different VR systems may have varying latency or bandwidth requirements, so optimizing the networking layer is key for smooth multiplayer experiences.

3. **Testing and Optimization**:

o **Continuous Testing on Multiple Devices**: It's important to test the game on all targeted platforms regularly to catch any platform-specific issues early. Testing should include verifying that all interactions, visual quality, and performance meet the expectations for each platform.

o **Optimization for Lower-End Devices**: Use tools like **Unreal's GPU Profiler** and **stat commands** to check the performance on standalone VR devices and adjust settings as needed. Pay close attention to the **frame rate** and **latency** to ensure that your game provides a smooth experience regardless of the platform.

Real-World Example: A Multiplayer VR Game That Works on Both Oculus Quest and HTC Vive

Let's explore a practical example of a VR game that works on both the **Oculus Quest** and **HTC Vive**. Consider a **multiplayer VR social game** that allows users to interact in a shared virtual space, play mini-games, and communicate through voice chat.

1. **Scenario Setup**:

    o The game includes a series of mini-games, such as VR bowling, racing, and a virtual escape room, which require real-time interaction between players.

- o The game has been designed to work across both **Oculus Quest** (standalone VR) and **HTC Vive** (PC VR), allowing players on either system to join the same session, interact, and play together.

2. **Step 1: Cross-Platform Input Handling**:

- o The game uses **abstracted input mappings** for controllers. For example, the **Oculus Touch controllers** and **Vive controllers** are mapped to the same in-game actions like grabbing, throwing, and interacting with objects. This ensures that players on different platforms can use their controllers without issues.

- o **Voice chat** is handled using Unreal's **online subsystem**, which supports communication across both devices, allowing players to talk to each other regardless of the headset they are using.

3. **Step 2: Dynamic Graphics Settings**:

- o The game has a **dynamic graphics quality system** that adjusts settings based on the platform. On the **HTC Vive**, players enjoy **higher-resolution textures**, **advanced post-processing effects**, and **real-time lighting**. On the **Oculus Quest**, the game automatically reduces texture quality and uses **baked lighting** to maintain smooth performance without compromising immersion.

4. **Step 3: UI/UX Design**:

   o The UI elements are designed to be responsive to both platforms. For example, the virtual menus and game controls are **scalable** so that they look appropriately sized for both the **Vive's higher-resolution screen** and the **Quest's lower-resolution display**.

   o The **VR UI system** uses **widgets** that adjust based on the headset's resolution, ensuring the user interface feels natural and responsive on all platforms.

5. **Step 4: Cross-Platform Multiplayer**:

   o The multiplayer system is built using **Unreal's networking tools**. Players using the **Oculus Quest** and **HTC Vive** are able to join the same virtual room without issues. The server manages the synchronization of game states, ensuring that both players see the same things in real time, regardless of their platform.

   o The **voice chat system** is integrated into the game, ensuring that players can communicate clearly regardless of whether they're using a standalone or PC VR system.

6. **Step 5: Testing and Optimization**:

- o Extensive playtesting is performed to ensure that the game works smoothly across both the **Oculus Quest** and **HTC Vive**. Optimizations are made for lower-end systems like the Quest, ensuring that the game runs at a stable **72 FPS** or **90 FPS** on all platforms.

- o Performance profiling is conducted using **Unreal's profiler tools**, and adjustments are made to optimize network bandwidth, latency, and frame rates for seamless multiplayer experiences.

This chapter provided an in-depth look at **building for different VR platforms**, focusing on the differences between **PC VR** and **standalone VR**, as well as how to handle **cross-platform development**. The **real-world example of a multiplayer VR game** demonstrated how to create a seamless, engaging experience across platforms, ensuring that performance, input handling, and multiplayer features work smoothly on both **Oculus Quest** and **HTC Vive**. By understanding the unique characteristics of each VR platform and optimizing your game for each, you can create a broader, more accessible VR experience.

CHAPTER 17

OPTIMIZING FOR MOBILE VR

Mobile VR Basics: Understanding the Limitations and Benefits of Mobile VR

Mobile VR refers to virtual reality experiences that run on standalone devices, such as smartphones or mobile VR headsets like **Google Cardboard** and **Samsung Gear VR**. These platforms offer a more accessible and affordable VR experience compared to PC-powered systems like the HTC Vive or Oculus Rift. However, mobile VR comes with its own set of limitations and benefits that developers need to understand to create optimal experiences.

1. **Limitations of Mobile VR**:
   - o **Hardware Constraints**: Mobile VR relies on smartphones for processing power, which are typically less powerful than PCs or consoles. This means mobile VR experiences need to be optimized to run on devices with lower processing capabilities, limited RAM, and less powerful GPUs.

- For example, smartphones generally have less processing power than dedicated VR headsets like the Oculus Rift, making it difficult to handle high-fidelity graphics and complex game mechanics.

o **Battery Life**: VR experiences on mobile devices can be battery-intensive, leading to shorter play sessions before the device needs to be recharged. Developers must design experiences that minimize battery drain, ensuring longer engagement.

o **Limited Input Methods**: Mobile VR typically uses either **motion controllers** (such as those for Gear VR) or **smartphone sensors** (for Google Cardboard), both of which offer less precision compared to the highly advanced controllers in PC VR setups. Interaction with the environment in mobile VR is generally limited to looking and tapping.

o **Field of View and Resolution**: Mobile VR headsets often have a lower field of view and resolution compared to PC-based systems. This can affect immersion and the level of detail you can provide in your environment. For instance, a phone's screen resolution may not provide the same sharpness and clarity as a high-end PC VR headset.

2. **Benefits of Mobile VR**:

   o **Affordability and Accessibility**: One of the biggest advantages of mobile VR is its **low cost** and widespread accessibility. Devices like **Google Cardboard** or **Gear VR** are inexpensive, making it easier for users to experience VR without needing expensive hardware or a powerful gaming PC.

   o **Portability**: Mobile VR is portable, allowing users to enjoy VR anywhere, as long as they have the headset and a compatible smartphone. This portability makes it ideal for casual VR experiences.

   o **Ease of Use**: Mobile VR headsets are easy to set up and use, making them beginner-friendly. Most mobile VR systems simply require inserting a smartphone into the headset, reducing the need for complex configuration or installation.

   o **Wider Audience Reach**: Since mobile VR is available on a variety of smartphones (iOS and Android), developers can reach a large and diverse audience, making it easier to distribute VR apps at scale.

Performance Tips for Mobile VR: How to Optimize for Lower-End Devices

Optimizing for mobile VR is essential to ensure a smooth, immersive experience, even on devices with limited resources. Developers need to consider multiple factors when building for mobile VR to balance performance and visual quality.

1. **Optimize Graphics and Assets**:
    o **Lower-Resolution Textures**: High-resolution textures may look fantastic on powerful PCs, but they can cause performance issues on mobile VR. Use **lower-resolution textures** for objects, particularly those in the background or far from the player's viewpoint.
    o **Simplify Models and Meshes**: Reduce the complexity of 3D models and mesh detail. Use **low-poly models** for background objects or environmental assets that are not central to the player's interaction. Mobile devices do not have the computational power to handle complex meshes without causing frame rate drops.
    o **Efficient Shaders**: Avoid complex shaders that require high processing power. Use simpler shaders for things like lighting, reflections, and textures to improve frame rate without sacrificing immersion.

    o **Static Objects**: Minimize the use of dynamic lighting and shadows. Where possible, use **baked lighting** for static objects to reduce computational load. This will also improve visual performance in VR.

2. **Frame Rate and Latency**:

    o **Target 60 FPS**: While high-end VR experiences often target **90 FPS** or higher, mobile VR should target a lower, but still steady **60 FPS** for smoother performance. Mobile devices have limited power, so ensuring a stable frame rate is essential for comfort and preventing motion sickness.

    o **Reduce Latency**: Latency can be particularly problematic in mobile VR, as it affects the responsiveness of the virtual environment. Keep latency as low as possible by reducing the number of assets and processing requirements that need to be loaded at any given moment.

3. **Optimize for Battery Life**:

    o **Reduce High-Performance Features**: Features like **high-resolution textures, complex physics,** and **real-time lighting** can be battery-intensive. These should be optimized or disabled for mobile VR to save power and improve battery life.

- o **Lower Screen Brightness**: The screen brightness can be a significant battery drainer, especially for extended VR sessions. While this might affect the visual quality slightly, consider giving the user an option to lower brightness to save battery.

4. **Optimize Input Methods**:

   - o **Simple Interactions**: Limit interactions to simple, natural input methods. Mobile VR headsets typically use **head-tracking** and **touchpad** or **motion controller** inputs, so avoid complex input systems that require precise controller movements.

   - o **Gesture Controls**: If available, use **gesture-based controls** (such as swiping, tapping, or pointing) to enhance immersion while keeping interactions simple. For example, tapping the touchpad on the headset could trigger a selection or object interaction, while head-tracking could control menus or item selection.

5. **Adaptive Quality Settings**:

   - o **Scalable Graphics Options**: Provide in-app settings that allow users to adjust graphics quality depending on their device's performance. This could include toggling between **low, medium, and high** graphics options. This flexibility

165

ensures that the game runs smoothly on a wide range of devices.

- o **Device Detection**: Detect the performance capabilities of the user's device and adjust settings accordingly. For instance, lower-end devices might automatically switch to lower texture resolutions or simpler lighting, while more powerful devices can support higher quality visuals.

6. **Optimizing for VR Comfort**:

- o **Minimize Motion Sickness**: Mobile VR can be more prone to **motion sickness** due to lower frame rates and lower processing power. Minimize **camera shakes, rapid movements**, and **fast rotations** that can lead to discomfort.

- o **Comfort Options**: Provide users with comfort options such as **teleportation** for movement instead of smooth locomotion, and use **static camera angles** when necessary to avoid causing nausea.

Real-World Example: Creating a Simple Mobile VR App for Cardboard or Gear VR

Let's walk through an example of creating a simple mobile VR app for **Google Cardboard** or **Samsung Gear VR**. This example will focus on optimizing the app for lower-end devices while maintaining an enjoyable user experience.

1. **Scenario Setup**:
   - The app is a **simple VR environment** where users can explore a virtual art gallery. The goal is to create an experience that runs smoothly on both low-end and mid-range mobile VR headsets, like Google Cardboard and Gear VR.

2. **Step 1: Optimizing Graphics for Mobile VR**:
   - **Textures**: The virtual art gallery is designed with minimal textures—most of the artwork is simple 2D images. The walls, floors, and ceiling have low-resolution textures, around 512x512 pixels, to ensure smooth performance.
   - **Low-Poly Models**: The art gallery is built with low-poly models, with a simple design for objects like shelves, pedestals, and frames. This reduces the strain on the mobile device's GPU.
   - **Baked Lighting**: Instead of using real-time lighting, the lighting and shadows are baked into the environment, providing static lightmaps that don't require additional processing power.

3. **Step 2: Achieving Smooth Frame Rates**:
   - **60 FPS Target**: The game targets a steady **60 FPS** on both Cardboard and Gear VR, ensuring smooth performance. The player is moving

slowly through the gallery, using head tracking to look at artwork, which helps maintain a low processing load.

o **Reduced Latency**: Head movement is tracked and synchronized quickly to avoid lag or disorienting stutter, crucial for VR comfort.

4. **Step 3: Simplified Input Methods**:

o **Cardboard**: On **Google Cardboard**, users interact by tapping the screen to navigate through the gallery. A simple **head gaze** system is used to select options or move between rooms, with minimal hand interaction.

o **Gear VR**: On **Samsung Gear VR**, users can use the touchpad on the side of the headset to move around or interact with objects. Simple gestures like **swiping** and **tapping** are implemented for easy navigation.

5. **Step 4: Optimizing for Battery Life**:

o **Reduced Screen Brightness**: The app provides an option to lower screen brightness, saving battery life while still ensuring a good viewing experience.

o **Efficient Power Management**: Background services that might consume power (such as heavy animations) are reduced or disabled to extend the device's battery life during extended play sessions.

6. **Step 5: Testing and Refining**:

   o **Cross-Device Testing**: The app is tested on multiple devices, from budget smartphones to mid-range devices, to ensure that performance is consistent across the board. Adjustments are made as necessary to optimize performance on the lowest spec devices.

   o **Playtesting**: Extensive playtesting is done to ensure that the user interface is intuitive, comfortable, and does not induce motion sickness, even on lower-end mobile VR headsets.

This chapter covered the **basics of mobile VR**, the **challenges and limitations** associated with these platforms, and provided **optimization tips** to ensure smooth, immersive experiences. By creating a **simple VR app for Google Cardboard or Gear VR**, we demonstrated how to optimize for performance, graphics, and interaction while ensuring a high-quality user experience on mobile VR platforms. Understanding and applying these principles will help developers build compelling VR experiences that run efficiently on mobile devices.

CHAPTER 18

USER COMFORT AND SAFETY IN VR

Reducing VR Fatigue: Techniques to Avoid Player Discomfort During Extended Play

One of the biggest challenges in VR development is ensuring that players remain comfortable and do not experience fatigue or discomfort during extended play sessions. VR fatigue can be caused by a variety of factors, such as poor performance, unnatural movements, or prolonged exposure to intense visuals. It is crucial for developers to prioritize comfort to keep players engaged without causing them physical or mental strain.

1. **Frame Rate and Latency**:
   o **Maintain a Steady Frame Rate**: One of the main causes of discomfort in VR is a **low frame rate**. Dropping below the recommended **90 FPS** can lead to motion sickness and discomfort. This is particularly important in VR, where even small frame rate drops can cause disorientation and nausea. Developers should optimize their games to consistently maintain a high frame rate,

especially in fast-moving or action-heavy sequences.

o **Reduce Latency**: High latency (the time it takes for the system to respond to player input) can make movements feel delayed or disconnected from what the player is seeing. To minimize latency, ensure efficient data transfer and keep system resources optimized, especially when dealing with multiplayer interactions or remote assets.

2. **Smooth and Comfortable Movement**:

o **Avoid Rapid Movement**: Rapid movements or sudden changes in direction can trigger motion sickness, especially if they don't match the player's head movement. Instead, implement movement options that are more comfortable for users, such as **teleportation** (where players jump to a new location) instead of smooth walking or running.

o **Comfort Options**: Many VR games allow users to toggle comfort options, such as a **vignette effect** (a black border that limits peripheral vision), reducing the intensity of movement. Implement options for users to customize their experience based on their comfort preferences.

- Adjusting Speed and Sensitivity: Make sure players can adjust movement speed and control sensitivity, which can reduce the feeling of imbalance or vertigo.

3. **Frequent Breaks and Play Sessions**:
   - **Encourage Breaks**: Long VR sessions can cause physical discomfort due to eye strain, neck pain, or motion fatigue. Consider implementing reminders or **timeout prompts** that encourage players to take a break after a certain period.
   - **Session Length Management**: VR experiences should be designed to offer short, engaging sessions rather than long periods of continuous play. Games or apps with shorter, bite-sized experiences can prevent players from overexerting themselves and becoming fatigued.

4. **Comfortable Visuals**:
   - **Eye Comfort**: Prolonged use of VR headsets can lead to eye strain, especially if the player is staring at a fixed point for an extended period. To reduce eye strain, avoid using bright, flashing lights or high-contrast colors that might stress the eyes.
   - **Adjustable FOV (Field of View)**: Some players may feel more comfortable with a wider or narrower field of view. Providing the ability to

adjust the FOV can help tailor the VR experience to the individual's needs and improve comfort.

5. **Adjusting the VR Environment**:

    o **Consistent and Familiar Navigation**: Use natural, intuitive movement methods for navigation. For example, walking or stepping in place is a natural movement for players and can reduce fatigue. Avoid disorienting movement methods like sudden jerks or disjointed camera movements.

Safety Measures: Setting Up Play Areas and Safe Zones

Player safety is paramount in VR, especially since VR experiences require physical movement within the play area. Without proper guidance and precautions, players could risk bumping into objects, tripping, or injuring themselves. Developers need to integrate safety features into their VR applications and ensure players are aware of their physical surroundings.

1. **Setting Up Play Areas**:

    o **Room-Scale VR Setup**: For devices like the **HTC Vive** or **Oculus Rift**, players need a **clear and spacious area** to move around in. Before using the VR headset, players should be guided to set up a **safe play zone** that is free from obstacles.

- The system often uses sensors or cameras to track the player's movement and will alert them if they are approaching the boundaries of the play area.

o **Boundaries and Warning Systems**: Ensure that your VR experience integrates boundary warning systems, which alert the player when they are approaching the edge of their play area. This can be done through visual cues (such as a grid or wall appearing in the virtual space) or haptic feedback on the controllers.

o **Clear Floor Space**: In games where players are encouraged to move around (such as dancing or exercising), make sure the player has **adequate floor space** to avoid bumping into furniture or other objects.

2. **Safe Zones and Virtual Boundaries**:

o **Guardian Systems**: Many VR headsets come with built-in **guardian systems** that create a virtual fence around the play area. This virtual fence prevents players from accidentally walking into walls or furniture by displaying warnings when they get too close to the edge.

- o **Safe Zones**: In VR environments that require movement, it's important to define "safe zones" where players can interact without risking injury. These zones can be either real (like a physical room) or virtual (like a designated area within the game world where players can safely engage in activities).

3. **Physical Safety**:
    - o **Encourage Proper Posture**: In VR fitness apps, make sure to encourage players to maintain **proper posture** to avoid strain or injury. For example, using virtual mirrors or visual guides to help players understand their posture can improve form and reduce injury risk.
    - o **Motion Safety**: Avoid rapid, jerky motions that could cause the player to trip or fall. Make sure movements are fluid and that players have enough space to move around naturally.

4. **User Control and Safety Preferences**:
    - o **Customizable Safety Features**: Allow users to control safety settings, such as enabling a boundary alert or adjusting the **play area size**. By giving users control, they can adjust safety measures based on their available space or preferences.

o **Session Time Limits**: In VR fitness or other physically demanding experiences, developers can build in time limits for activity, alerting users to take breaks at regular intervals.

Real-World Example: Designing a Comfortable Experience in VR Fitness Applications

Let's consider the example of a **VR fitness application** like **Supernatural** or **Beat Saber**, where players engage in physical activity using VR. These apps demand movement, sometimes intense, which could lead to discomfort or fatigue if not properly optimized for comfort and safety.

1. **Scenario Setup**:
   o The game involves a series of activities that require the player to move their arms, legs, or body to interact with virtual objects, hit targets, or follow exercise routines. These activities can be physically demanding, and the VR experience needs to be designed with player comfort and safety in mind.
2. **Step 1: Reducing Fatigue**:
   o The app includes **adjustable intensity settings**, allowing players to choose between light,

moderate, or intense workouts based on their comfort levels.

- o **Break Reminders**: The app includes reminders for players to take breaks every 15–20 minutes to reduce strain and ensure they don't overexert themselves during a workout.

- o **Stretching and Warm-Up Guides**: Prior to starting a workout, players are guided through a brief **warm-up routine** to prepare their bodies for the movements. This reduces the risk of injury and helps prevent fatigue.

3. **Step 2: Safe Play Area Setup**:

- o The app integrates the **guardian system** on the **Oculus Quest 2**, so players are warned when they are approaching the boundary of their play area.

- o If the user is about to move out of the safe zone, a visual cue (e.g., a grid or glowing boundary) appears to alert them.

- o **Floor Space Recommendations**: The game encourages players to ensure they have **at least 3–5 feet of clear space** in front of them to move their arms and legs without obstacles.

4. **Step 3: Physical Comfort**:

- o **Tracking Posture**: The app includes a virtual mirror that helps players monitor their posture while performing movements. This is particularly useful for preventing improper form during exercises, which could lead to discomfort or injury.

- o **Reducing Motion Sickness**: The game incorporates **smooth, controlled movements** and offers options like **teleportation** or **snap-turning** for users who are sensitive to motion sickness.

5. **Step 4: Monitoring Player Health**:

- o The VR fitness app integrates with **heart rate monitors** (via Bluetooth devices) or smartphone sensors to monitor the player's heart rate. Based on this data, the game can adjust the workout intensity in real-time, ensuring that players stay within a safe zone and don't overexert themselves.

- o **Hydration and Rest Reminders**: The app sends periodic notifications to encourage players to hydrate or rest after intense sessions, improving long-term comfort and safety.

This chapter covered **user comfort and safety** in VR, highlighting strategies for reducing **VR fatigue**, creating **safe play areas**, and implementing features that prioritize user well-being. The example of a **VR fitness application** demonstrated how to design comfortable, engaging, and safe VR experiences by considering aspects like movement intensity, user preferences, and environmental safety. By integrating these principles, developers can create immersive VR experiences that are enjoyable and sustainable for players over long periods of play.

CHAPTER 19

VR DEVELOPMENT BEST PRACTICES

Usability Testing in VR: Methods for Testing User Experiences in VR

Usability testing is a critical part of developing any VR experience. Since VR is a highly immersive and interactive medium, testing the user experience (UX) in real-world conditions is essential to ensure comfort, engagement, and usability. Unlike traditional testing, VR requires special attention to how players interact with the virtual environment and how comfortable and intuitive those interactions are.

1. **Types of Usability Testing**:
   o **Exploratory Testing**: This type of testing involves giving users an early version of the VR application and observing their natural interaction with it. The goal is to identify areas where players may be confused, frustrated, or disengaged. It's important to watch for signs of discomfort, such as **physical strain, motion sickness,** or **difficulty with controls**.

- o **Task-Based Testing**: In this test, users are asked to perform specific tasks within the VR environment (e.g., grabbing an object, moving through an environment, completing a mini-game). Observing how users accomplish these tasks can highlight areas where the interface or controls might need improvement.

- o **Controlled Experiments**: These tests are more structured and focus on specific variables, such as testing the effectiveness of certain design elements (e.g., menu navigation, movement style, or UI layout). You can control variables like the type of input method (controller, hand tracking, gaze control) and compare how users react to different designs.

2. **Key Considerations During Usability Testing**:

- o **Motion Sickness and Fatigue**: VR can induce **motion sickness**, especially when there are issues like frame rate drops, lag, or disjointed movement. Test the comfort level of your experience by tracking signs of nausea, dizziness, or eye strain during prolonged sessions.

- o **User Comfort**: Ensure that users don't experience physical discomfort, such as neck strain, eye fatigue, or poor posture. Keep in mind that VR can require significant body movement, so consider the ergonomics of the interactions (e.g., excessive hand or head movements).

- o **Feedback from Sensory Systems**: VR testing involves more than just observing visual and audio feedback; it's crucial to assess **haptic feedback, motion tracking,** and **gesture recognition** to ensure they feel responsive and natural.

3. **Testing Tools**:

- o **Eye Tracking**: Some headsets like the **Oculus Quest 2** or **HTC Vive Pro** have **eye-tracking capabilities**. Eye tracking can help you identify where users are focusing their attention in the VR environment and reveal potential issues with UI placement or environment design.

- o **Motion Capture**: Using motion capture systems to track user movements can provide data on how natural and comfortable the movement is in VR. This data can be used to optimize locomotion mechanics or interaction gestures.

4. **Remote Usability Testing**:

- o With the growth of VR, remote testing has become more common. Developers can perform **remote usability testing** by using screen-sharing or **VR streaming** technologies to observe users in real-time. This allows testers to gather insights without being physically present, saving time and cost.

Player Feedback and Iteration: How to Incorporate Feedback into Your VR Project

User feedback is invaluable in the iterative process of VR development. Players' thoughts, feelings, and experiences provide key insights into how the game or app can be improved. Incorporating feedback helps identify areas where the VR experience may be falling short and where improvements can be made to enhance immersion, usability, and comfort.

1. **Methods of Collecting Player Feedback**:
   - **Surveys and Questionnaires**: After a testing session, surveys or questionnaires can help collect structured feedback from players. Questions can range from quantitative (e.g., "How comfortable was the movement?" on a scale from 1 to 10) to qualitative (e.g., "What did you find frustrating about the experience?").
   - **In-Game Feedback Systems**: Integrate a **feedback system directly within the VR experience**, allowing users to submit feedback on their interactions in real time. This can include

simple thumbs-up/thumbs-down systems, satisfaction ratings, or more detailed comments.

- o **Player Observations**: Conducting live testing where players are observed while they play can provide insights that surveys alone cannot. Pay attention to how they interact with the environment, what actions seem confusing, and where they struggle the most.

- o **Focus Groups**: Bringing together a group of players after they've played the game and facilitating a **focus group discussion** can provide more in-depth feedback. Players can discuss their likes, dislikes, and suggestions for improvement.

2. **Incorporating Feedback into Your VR Project**:

- o **Analyze Feedback**: Collecting feedback is only useful if it's carefully analyzed and prioritized. Look for common themes across player responses, such as difficulties with specific controls or parts of the environment that are confusing. This allows you to focus on the most critical issues that affect the user experience.

- o **Prioritize Changes**: Based on the feedback, prioritize what changes need to be made first. This could be tweaking the movement mechanics, improving the UI, or addressing comfort issues like motion sickness. Prioritize the changes that will have the most significant impact on user comfort and enjoyment.

- o **Prototyping and Iteration**: After implementing changes, test the updates with the same group of users (or a new group). This process of **rapid prototyping and iteration** helps ensure that the changes made are beneficial and do not introduce new issues.

- o **Incorporating Positive Feedback**: Don't just focus on criticism. Pay attention to what players enjoy about the experience and what aspects are working well. This positive feedback can serve as the foundation for reinforcing those elements and expanding them.

3. **Implementing Iteration Cycles**:

- o **Continuous Iteration**: VR development is an iterative process that never truly stops. After every round of testing and feedback collection, take the time to update the game and test again. **Short, frequent iteration cycles** are key to improving the overall quality of the experience.

- o **Community Involvement**: In some cases, especially with ongoing VR projects, involving the player community in testing can be beneficial. Allowing players to be part of the development process and hear their thoughts on new features or fixes can create a more engaged user base.

Real-World Example: Using User Feedback to Refine a VR Game

Let's look at an example of using player feedback to refine a VR game, such as a **VR puzzle game** that's being developed for the Oculus Quest. Early testing shows that players are struggling with the interaction mechanics, particularly when trying to pick up and place objects within the puzzle environment.

1. **Scenario Setup**:
   o In this VR puzzle game, players are tasked with solving increasingly complex puzzles by interacting with virtual objects. The game uses hand tracking for object manipulation, and players are expected to move and arrange pieces using natural gestures.

2. **Step 1: Initial User Testing and Feedback Collection**:
   o During the first round of testing, players report feeling **frustrated** with the accuracy of the hand tracking. Objects are difficult to pick up, and players often drop or misplace pieces. Some players also express discomfort with the amount of time they have to hold an object in place to interact with it.

    o   In a follow-up survey, users also mention that the UI elements are hard to see and interact with, especially in the game's low-light environments.

3. **Step 2: Analyzing Feedback and Prioritizing Changes**:
   - o   After analyzing the feedback, the development team identifies two major pain points:
     1. **Hand tracking accuracy**: Many players experience difficulty in manipulating objects because the hand tracking isn't precise enough.
     2. **UI visibility**: The interface is too subtle, especially in darker environments, leading to confusion.
   - o   The team decides to focus on improving hand tracking accuracy first, as this directly impacts the core gameplay mechanics.

4. **Step 3: Iterating on the Game**:
   - o   The development team makes several updates:
     - ▪ **Improved hand tracking**: The team tweaks the gesture recognition system, adding more precise hand positioning algorithms and including a **visual cue** (like a glow effect) to indicate when an object can be picked up or manipulated.
     - ▪ **UI Improvements**: The UI is adjusted to make it brighter and more prominent in

low-light conditions. The team also introduces an **object-focused UI**, making it easier for players to see and interact with menu items or settings.

5. **Step 4: Testing the Changes**:

   o A new round of testing is conducted to assess how players respond to the updates. Players report improved accuracy with hand tracking and find the UI much easier to navigate. The game feels more intuitive, and the gameplay experience is smoother and more enjoyable.

6. **Step 5: Final Adjustments**:

   o The team continues testing and refining the game, using additional player feedback to make smaller tweaks to the game world, movement mechanics, and difficulty curve. Through continuous iteration, the game evolves into a polished and highly engaging VR experience.

This chapter discussed **usability testing** and the importance of **incorporating player feedback** to improve VR experiences. By conducting effective usability testing, gathering user input, and iterating based on feedback, developers can ensure their VR projects are intuitive, immersive, and comfortable. The real-world example of using feedback to refine a **VR puzzle game** demonstrated how feedback can be leveraged to improve core gameplay mechanics, UI design, and overall user experience. By continually refining your VR experience based on user feedback, you can create a more engaging and enjoyable product for players.

CHAPTER 20

MARKETING YOUR VR EXPERIENCE

Building a VR Portfolio: Showcasing Your VR Projects to Potential Clients

Creating a strong portfolio is essential for any VR developer looking to attract potential clients, collaborators, or investors. Your VR portfolio should demonstrate your skills, creativity, and the value you can bring to a project, whether you're working independently or as part of a studio.

1. **What to Include in Your VR Portfolio**:
    o   **Diverse Range of Projects**: Show a variety of VR experiences that highlight different skills and applications. For example, include a mix of games, simulations, educational applications, and interactive experiences. This will demonstrate your versatility as a VR developer.
    o   **High-Quality Demos**: A well-polished **demo reel** is essential. Include short video clips or interactive demos of your VR projects. The videos should focus on key aspects like

190

interaction mechanics, user experience, and immersion. Ensure that the demo highlights the core strengths of each project.

- o **Project Descriptions**: For each project in your portfolio, include a brief description that outlines the goal, the technology used, and the challenges you overcame. Highlight your contributions to the project, whether it's programming, design, or creative direction.

- o **Interactive VR Demos**: When possible, allow potential clients to experience your VR projects firsthand. Providing access to interactive demos—either in-person or via cloud-based solutions (such as **Oculus Link** or **SteamVR**)— can be a powerful way to showcase your work.

2. **Online Portfolio**:

- o **Website or Dedicated Platform**: Hosting your portfolio on your own website or a platform like **ArtStation** or **Behance** allows easy access for potential clients. Ensure your website is mobile-friendly and has clear, easy-to-navigate sections, such as demos, project descriptions, and your contact details.

- o **Social Media Presence**: Social media platforms, particularly those that emphasize visual content, like **Instagram** and **YouTube**, are great ways to showcase VR work. Posting demo videos or behind-the-scenes content can engage a wider audience and attract clients who are looking for specific VR expertise.

3. **Highlight Client Testimonials and Collaborations**:

   o If you've worked on projects for clients or have collaborated with other VR studios, include **testimonials** or **case studies** in your portfolio. Client feedback or a successful collaboration speaks volumes about your professionalism and the value of your work.

   o Share any **press coverage**, **awards**, or **recognitions** related to your VR projects. These can be a great selling point when marketing your skills to potential clients.

Promoting VR Games and Apps: Best Practices for Marketing VR Content

Marketing VR content requires a tailored approach, as the audience for VR experiences is unique, and the technology is still growing. The key is to focus on **immersion, engagement**, and **experience** to make your content stand out in a competitive market.

1. **Understand Your Target Audience**:

- o **Identify the VR Enthusiasts**: VR games and apps typically appeal to tech-savvy users who are eager to explore new forms of entertainment. Your marketing strategy should focus on this audience, creating campaigns that emphasize innovation, interactivity, and immersion.

- o **Identify Niche Markets**: Not all VR experiences need to be games. Some VR apps are designed for **education, healthcare, virtual tourism**, or **training**. Identifying the specific **niche** that your VR content caters to can help you market directly to those interested in those industries.

2. **Leverage Social Media**:

- o **Platform-Specific Content**: Different platforms serve different purposes, so tailor your content accordingly:

  - ▪ **Instagram**: Share stunning visuals, VR gameplay clips, or teaser videos that show the immersive nature of your VR experience.

  - ▪ **YouTube**: Create **trailers, gameplay videos**, or **dev diaries** that offer a behind-the-scenes look at your development process. You can also collaborate with VR content creators to promote your game.

- **Facebook/Twitter**: These platforms can be used for updates, behind-the-scenes posts, and user engagement. Facebook groups and Twitter hashtags (like **#VR** and **#VRgames**) can help increase visibility.

3. **Create a Compelling Demo**:
   o **Free Trials**: Allow potential users to experience a **short demo** of your VR game or app. Offering a free version can help attract a larger audience and give them a taste of the immersive experience. This can also encourage them to purchase the full version of the game or app.

   o **Steam Early Access or Oculus Store Demo**: Platforms like **Steam** and the **Oculus Store** allow developers to release demos or early access versions. This helps you gauge user feedback, fix bugs, and build anticipation.

4. **Collaborate with Influencers**:
   o **Partner with VR Content Creators**: Reach out to VR YouTubers, streamers, and social media influencers to create promotional content for your game or app. Influencers have a dedicated following and can provide in-depth reviews and exposure to your VR project.

- o **Review Sites and Communities**: There are many dedicated VR review websites and forums, such as **Road to VR**, **UploadVR**, and **Reddit's r/virtualreality**. Submitting your game for review can attract interest and get your content in front of a more specialized audience.

5. **Attend VR and Gaming Events**:

- o **Showcase at Conferences and Expos**: Events like **GDC (Game Developers Conference)**, **Oculus Connect**, and **CES** (Consumer Electronics Show) are prime opportunities for showcasing your VR game to industry professionals, press, and potential clients. Presenting a demo at such events can increase exposure and generate buzz.

- o **Competitions and Awards**: Consider entering VR-related competitions or applying for industry awards. Winning or being nominated for an award can greatly increase your visibility and credibility.

6. **Email Marketing**:

- o **Build an Email List**: Collect email addresses from interested users, whether through your website or at events. Regularly update them on development progress, upcoming releases, and special offers.

o **Newsletters and Updates**: Keep your audience engaged with periodic newsletters that provide updates, release notes, and upcoming events. Offering exclusive content or discounts for email subscribers can encourage sign-ups.

Real-World Example: How a VR Studio Successfully Marketed Its VR Experience to a Wide Audience

Let's take a look at a real-world example of how a VR studio successfully marketed its VR experience, focusing on **Beat Games** and their popular VR game **Beat Saber**, a rhythm-based VR game available on platforms like Oculus, PSVR, and Steam.

1. **Scenario Setup**:
   o **Beat Saber** is a rhythm game that has players use lightsabers to slice through cubes representing musical beats. With its simple mechanics and immersive experience, the game quickly gained popularity in the VR community.
2. **Step 1: Leveraging Social Media and Influencers**:
   o **YouTube and Twitch**: Beat Games partnered with well-known YouTubers and streamers to showcase the game in action. Influencers like **PewDiePie** and VR-focused streamers created viral content that exposed the game to a massive

audience. Streamers' gameplay videos generated organic interest and sparked conversations about the game.

- ○ **Social Media Content**: The studio shared high-quality gameplay trailers, updates, and behind-the-scenes content across social media platforms like Instagram, Twitter, and Facebook. They regularly engaged with their audience by sharing fan-created content, which created a sense of community.

3. **Step 2: Building Hype with Pre-Launch and Early Access**:
   - ○ **Early Access on Steam**: Beat Games initially released the game on **Steam Early Access**. This allowed them to collect player feedback, make improvements, and build a fanbase before the official release. The studio used early access as an opportunity to refine the game and build hype.
   - ○ **Demo at Events**: Beat Games showcased Beat Saber at major gaming events like **PAX** and **E3**, where players could try the game firsthand. The exposure at these events helped build anticipation for the full release.

4. **Step 3: Cross-Platform Release**:
   - ○ After the initial release, Beat Saber expanded to different VR platforms, including **Oculus Quest**

and **PSVR**, making the game accessible to a broader audience. They also continued to release **new music packs** and **free updates** that kept players engaged and encouraged them to keep playing.

5. **Step 4: Maintaining Engagement**:

    o   Beat Games consistently engaged with its community by adding new features, creating events, and listening to player feedback. They also provided **post-launch content** in the form of new music packs, exclusive content, and updates, which kept players returning to the game.

    o   The studio also **engaged directly** with players through social media, responding to queries, sharing updates, and encouraging fan interaction with contests and challenges.

6. **Step 5: Viral Growth and Global Reach**:

    o   Beat Saber's success was amplified through word of mouth, influencer partnerships, and the social media presence. The game became one of the **best-selling VR games** worldwide, attracting a large and diverse player base.

    o   The studio's consistent updates, social media interaction, and engagement with the community helped them build a loyal following and expand the game's reach.

This chapter explored the best practices for **marketing VR content**, from **building a compelling portfolio** to leveraging **social media, influencers, and early access**. The **real-world example of Beat Games and Beat Saber** demonstrated how strategic marketing, community engagement, and cross-platform availability can help a VR experience reach a wide audience. By following these best practices, you can build awareness for your VR projects and attract players or clients. Effective marketing is about telling a compelling story and creating a community around your experience.

CHAPTER 21

VR FOR TRAINING AND SIMULATION

Creating VR Simulations: Developing VR for Training in Fields Like Aviation, Medicine, and More

Virtual Reality (VR) has revolutionized various industries by providing immersive simulations that are both cost-effective and efficient for training purposes. VR enables learners to practice complex tasks and scenarios in a controlled virtual environment, where real-world consequences are avoided. This makes VR ideal for fields like aviation, healthcare, military training, and beyond.

1. **VR for Aviation Training**:
   o **Flight Simulators**: One of the most well-established uses of VR in training is in **aviation**. VR flight simulators allow pilots to practice complex maneuvers and emergency situations without the risks or costs associated with real-life training. VR simulators can replicate various flying conditions, from weather challenges (such as turbulence and storms) to emergency protocols (like engine failures or system malfunctions).

- o **Advantages**:
  - **Cost-Effective**: Using VR for flight simulation eliminates the high costs of maintaining physical simulators and real aircraft.
  - **Realistic Training**: VR offers a realistic, immersive experience that allows trainees to practice scenarios they may not encounter frequently in real life, such as extreme weather conditions or mechanical failures.
  - **Instant Feedback**: Trainers can provide immediate feedback to students about their performance in the simulator, helping them improve skills faster.

2. **VR for Medical Training**:
   - o **Surgical Simulations**: VR is becoming an essential tool in **medical training**, particularly for **surgical procedures**. Virtual surgical simulators allow medical professionals to practice operations in a risk-free environment, enabling them to refine their skills and techniques before performing real surgeries. Surgeons can simulate various scenarios, such as operating on different types of patients or dealing with rare complications.

201

- o **Advantages**:
  - **Reduced Risk**: Trainees can practice surgeries without the risk of harming real patients.
  - **Repetitive Practice**: VR allows students to repeat procedures as often as necessary to gain proficiency.
  - **Accessible and Affordable**: VR-based training can make specialized education more accessible, especially for medical institutions that may not have access to high-cost simulators or cadaver labs.

3. **VR for Industrial and Military Training**:
   - o **Construction and Maintenance**: VR is being used in the **industrial sector** to train workers for construction and maintenance tasks. Simulations can replicate hazardous environments, enabling trainees to practice safety protocols and critical procedures.
   - o **Military Applications**: In the **military**, VR allows soldiers to undergo tactical and strategic training in realistic environments, including simulations of combat situations, navigation, and weapon handling. VR can also simulate **urban warfare** or **combat medical training**, helping

soldiers to build skills without the risks of live-fire exercises.

4. **VR for Corporate Training**:

   o **Employee Skill Development**: Many corporations are adopting VR for **employee training** in customer service, technical skills, leadership, and soft skills development. Virtual scenarios can be created for role-playing interactions, decision-making, and conflict resolution, making training more engaging and practical.

   o **Remote Training**: VR enables remote employees to participate in training sessions without needing to be physically present, which is particularly useful for global companies.

Assessment and Metrics in VR Training: Evaluating the Effectiveness of VR Simulations

Effective training requires not only high-quality VR simulations but also robust **assessment systems** to measure the learner's progress and ensure the training achieves its goals. Evaluating the effectiveness of VR training can be done through various metrics and tools that help assess performance, retention, and engagement.

1. **Tracking Performance**:
   - ○ **Real-Time Monitoring**: VR simulations should be designed to track **real-time performance metrics**. For example, in a medical training simulation, the system could track the accuracy of the trainee's movements during surgery (such as how well they use surgical tools or how precise their incisions are).
   - ○ **Key Performance Indicators (KPIs)**: Identify specific KPIs based on the task being trained. For example, in aviation training, KPIs might include **reaction time**, **accuracy of controls**, or **adherence to procedures** during emergency simulations.
   - ○ **Data Collection**: Collecting data such as **reaction times, decision-making processes**, and **task completion rates** provides objective insights into the learner's skills and areas for improvement.

2. **Simulated Scenarios and Decision-Making**:
   - ○ **Scenario-Based Testing**: In training simulations, you can present the trainee with a range of scenarios to assess their decision-making ability. For instance, in a medical VR training scenario, the system could evaluate the trainee's response

to emergency situations (e.g., handling a complication during surgery).

- o **Adaptive Difficulty**: Advanced VR training simulations can dynamically adjust their complexity based on the learner's performance. For example, if a trainee performs well in basic scenarios, the system can present more complex or high-pressure situations to test their limits and abilities.

3. **User Engagement and Retention**:

- o **Engagement Metrics**: Track user engagement levels by measuring how long users are interacting with the VR simulation and whether they exhibit consistent interest throughout the training session. High engagement typically correlates with better knowledge retention.

- o **Post-Training Evaluation**: To measure the effectiveness of the training, conduct assessments after the VR training to evaluate how well the learner retained and applied the knowledge or skills they gained. This could include written tests, hands-on demonstrations, or interviews.

- o **Comparative Analysis**: One of the best ways to gauge the effectiveness of VR training is by comparing pre- and post-training performance. For instance, a pilot trainee might perform an actual flight simulation before and after VR-based training to measure improvements in flight techniques and decision-making.

4. **Learning Analytics**:
   o Use **learning analytics** tools to aggregate data from the VR training sessions. By analyzing how users interact with the simulation, you can gather insights into where they struggle and what aspects of the training need improvement. These insights can help refine future training sessions and ensure that trainees are getting the most out of their experience.

5. **Feedback Loops**:
   o Implement **feedback loops** within the VR training experience. This allows the system to provide real-time feedback during the simulation, helping trainees make corrections or adjustments as they go. Feedback can be delivered through visual cues, haptic feedback, or voice prompts, and it helps keep trainees on track.

Real-World Example: The Use of VR in Medical Training or Pilot Simulators

To demonstrate how VR is applied in real-world training, let's explore two examples: **medical training** and **pilot simulators**.

1. **Medical Training with VR**:
    o **Example: Osso VR**: **Osso VR** is a medical VR training platform that allows surgeons and medical professionals to practice surgeries in a simulated, risk-free environment. Osso VR offers training for various procedures, including **laparoscopic surgery, orthopedic procedures**, and **spinal surgeries**.
        ▪ **Scenario Setup**: Surgeons use the VR headset to perform tasks like making incisions, handling surgical tools, and interacting with virtual patients. The system tracks their movements and provides **real-time feedback** on their technique.
        ▪ **Assessment**: The platform provides detailed performance analytics after each training session, evaluating key metrics like **accuracy, time taken**, and **tool handling**. It also offers reports that show progress over time, helping to identify areas where the surgeon may need further practice.
    o **Step 1: Performance Metrics**: The system tracks the accuracy of each incision, the speed at which the surgery is completed, and the overall

207

procedural flow. This provides an objective measurement of a trainee's skill.

- o **Step 2: Real-Time Feedback**: If the surgeon deviates from the correct procedure, the system immediately provides feedback (e.g., "You've missed the correct incision point, please adjust"). This is crucial for developing muscle memory and proper technique in medical procedures.

- o **Step 3: Adaptive Scenarios**: The platform presents increasingly complex scenarios as the user's skill improves. The system may simulate a **bleeding complication** during a procedure, requiring the surgeon to apply pressure and stop the bleeding.

2. **Pilot Simulators with VR**:

- o **Example: Redbird Flight Simulations**: Redbird offers VR-based flight simulators that help pilots practice maneuvers and emergency procedures in a safe, controlled environment. These simulators allow pilots to experience **bad weather conditions**, **system failures**, and other critical scenarios.

   - **Scenario Setup**: Pilots use VR headsets to simulate flying through turbulent conditions or handle emergency scenarios such as **engine failure** or **navigation malfunctions**.

- **Assessment**: The simulator tracks **reaction times, correctness of decisions**, and **handling of the aircraft**. It provides feedback on how well the pilot handles specific situations, with detailed post-flight debriefings to highlight mistakes and areas for improvement.

o **Step 1: Simulated Flight Conditions**: The VR system simulates various weather conditions, from thunderstorms to fog, giving pilots the experience of flying in challenging environments without leaving the ground.

o **Step 2: Emergency Simulations**: The pilot may experience **engine failure** mid-flight, forcing them to take corrective actions like finding a safe landing spot. The system tests their ability to handle high-pressure situations and adapt to unexpected circumstances.

o **Step 3: Post-Training Debrief**: After each session, the simulator provides a comprehensive report on the pilot's performance, including areas where they made the right decisions and areas that require improvement.

This chapter explored the application of **VR for training and simulation** in various fields, from **aviation and healthcare** to **military and industrial training**. We discussed the importance of **assessing and measuring** the effectiveness of VR training through performance tracking, user engagement, and real-time feedback. The real-world examples of **medical training** and **pilot simulators** demonstrated how VR is used to provide immersive, risk-free environments for practice and improvement. By leveraging VR, training programs can become more accessible, engaging, and effective in preparing individuals for real-world tasks and scenarios.

CHAPTER 22

THE FUTURE OF VR DEVELOPMENT

VR and AI Integration: How AI is Shaping the Future of VR

The integration of **Artificial Intelligence (AI)** with Virtual Reality (VR) is poised to redefine how we interact with and experience virtual environments. By bringing AI into the mix, developers can create more intelligent, responsive, and immersive VR experiences that adapt in real-time to user behavior and environmental changes. AI's role in VR is still evolving, and its future implications are vast.

1. **AI-Driven Interactions**:
    o AI allows for more **dynamic and intelligent non-playable characters (NPCs)** in VR. Instead of pre-programmed behaviors, NPCs can use machine learning algorithms to adapt their actions based on the player's behavior. For example, in a VR game, NPCs could recognize the player's actions and alter their responses, making the experience more engaging and less predictable.

- o **Procedural Content Generation**: AI can assist in generating realistic and varied environments and scenarios. In VR games or simulations, AI algorithms can dynamically generate content such as landscapes, missions, or quests based on a user's preferences and past behavior, creating a personalized experience.

- o **Natural Language Processing (NLP)**: By integrating **NLP** into VR experiences, players can interact with the virtual world through spoken commands or conversations with NPCs. For example, a player might speak to a VR character, and AI would understand and respond contextually, creating a more immersive experience.

2. **AI for Personalization**:

- o AI can analyze user behavior and preferences to tailor VR experiences, ensuring that each interaction feels unique and highly engaging. For example, a VR fitness application could use AI to adjust workout difficulty in real-time based on the user's performance or physical limitations, enhancing the training experience.

- o **Adaptive Learning**: AI can enable VR simulations to adapt to the skill level of the user. In educational applications, for instance, the system could provide more challenging content once a learner has mastered earlier concepts, ensuring constant engagement and growth.

3. **AI in VR for Automation**:

    o **AI-Driven Testing and Debugging**: AI can also be used in the **development phase** of VR projects to automate testing and bug detection. AI-powered systems can simulate a variety of interactions in a VR experience, identifying potential problems that might arise during real-world use, thus streamlining the development process.

    o **Behavioral Analytics**: AI can collect data on how users interact with VR environments, identifying pain points or areas where users are struggling. This data can then be used to make improvements to the design, controls, or overall experience.

The Role of AR: Augmented Reality's Influence on VR Development

While Virtual Reality (VR) immerses users in completely virtual worlds, **Augmented Reality (AR)** blends the digital world with the physical, superimposing virtual elements onto the real world. The fusion of AR and VR is creating a new realm of **mixed reality (MR)**, where the two technologies complement each other to enhance the user experience. The influence of AR on VR development is already visible, and this trend is only expected to grow in the future.

1. **Augmented Reality Enhancing VR**:
   - **Hybrid VR/AR Experiences**: VR and AR are increasingly being integrated into **mixed reality (MR)** environments, where users can interact with both real-world objects and virtual elements simultaneously. For example, in a training application, users might wear a VR headset, but see real-world objects augmented with virtual elements (such as instructions or visual cues) that enhance the training process.
   - **Real-World Data Integration**: AR can be used to overlay real-world information or objects into VR environments. For example, in a VR surgery simulation, AR might display additional contextual information, such as real-time vitals of a virtual patient, alongside the simulated environment, aiding in decision-making and enhancing immersion.

2. **AR and VR Collaboration in Gaming and Entertainment**:
   - **Immersive Interactive Environments**: Imagine a VR game where the physical space around the player is augmented with interactive objects. For

214

instance, the real walls of the room could be integrated into the virtual game world, allowing the player to touch, move, or interact with elements in both realms, creating a seamless experience.

- o **Enhanced Storytelling**: VR can use AR to create interactive narratives where players see real-world objects infused with digital content. For example, an AR app could allow users to experience a **virtual scavenger hunt** where they find and interact with virtual objects in their real environment using VR headsets.

3. **AR in Training and Simulation**:
   - o **Blended Reality in Education**: AR has the potential to bring real-world objects into VR simulations, enhancing learning in fields such as **architecture**, **medicine**, and **manufacturing**. For example, AR could allow trainees to interact with physical models or devices in their environment while receiving virtual guidance, feedback, or instructions.
   - o **Hands-On Interaction**: In VR training, AR could be used to highlight specific areas of focus or provide visual aids to help guide users through complex tasks. For example, in a VR car repair simulation, AR could highlight parts of the

vehicle that need to be repaired while providing virtual tools for the user to interact with.

4. **Improved UX and User Interaction**:

   o **AR Navigation**: While in VR, AR can provide additional layers of information to help users orient themselves within the virtual space. This could be particularly useful in complex environments, such as VR-based escape rooms or training simulators, where users may need a constant reminder of their goals or location.

   o **Enhancing Physical Interactions**: By integrating AR into VR systems, users can receive **real-time feedback** on their movements and interactions. For example, users could see virtual overlays in their field of view that show their physical gestures, making it easier to interact with the virtual world.

Real-World Example: Emerging Trends in Mixed Reality

The growing convergence of AR and VR has led to the rise of **mixed reality (MR)**, where the boundaries between the physical and digital worlds are increasingly blurred. Several companies are at the forefront of MR development, creating **innovative products** and experiences that demonstrate how the future of VR development will look when combined with AR.

1. **Example: Microsoft HoloLens**:

   o The **Microsoft HoloLens** is one of the most well-known MR devices, blending the power of AR and VR to create immersive experiences that are both interactive and context-aware. Unlike traditional VR headsets, HoloLens uses transparent lenses that allow users to see the real world while interacting with digital objects that are overlaid on top of it.

   o **Application in Industry**: HoloLens has been used in industries such as healthcare, construction, and manufacturing. In healthcare, for example, HoloLens allows surgeons to view 3D models of patients' organs during surgery, enhancing their understanding and improving precision. In construction, architects can use HoloLens to visualize designs within actual buildings, giving a real-time view of how new elements would integrate into existing structures.

   o **Emerging Trends**: The HoloLens has demonstrated the power of MR in bridging the gap between physical and virtual worlds, and its applications are only expanding as the device becomes more advanced. With **AI and machine learning** integrated into the system, users can experience more intelligent and personalized interactions, which will shape the future of VR and AR.

2. **Example: Magic Leap**:

   o **Magic Leap** is another leader in the MR field, using a combination of **AR and VR** to create immersive, interactive experiences. Their **Magic Leap 1** headset blends virtual objects with the real world, allowing users to interact with both digital and physical elements.

   o **Application in Entertainment**: Magic Leap has made strides in the entertainment industry by creating immersive gaming experiences that blend physical spaces with virtual content. For example, users can place virtual characters and objects in their real-world environment and interact with them in a fully immersive way.

   o **Emerging Trends**: Magic Leap is pushing the boundaries of interactive storytelling, where users not only watch a story unfold but also become part of it. As the technology improves, the integration of AI into MR platforms will allow for increasingly personalized and engaging experiences.

3. **Example: Varjo XR-3**:

   o **Varjo XR-3** is a mixed reality headset that provides **ultra-realistic experiences** by combining high-fidelity VR with AR, allowing users to interact with both virtual and physical worlds with unprecedented clarity. It's used in fields such as **aviation training**, **design**, and **engineering**.

- o **Real-World Applications**: The XR-3's advanced visual quality allows for detailed simulations that could replace traditional training methods. For instance, in aviation, pilots can train with real-world equipment while interacting with virtual environments for a comprehensive and cost-effective experience.

4. **Industry Applications and Future Impacts**:

- o As VR and AR technologies converge, the **mixed reality** sector will grow exponentially, with applications across numerous industries, including **education**, **healthcare**, **manufacturing**, and **entertainment**.

- o **AI-enhanced MR**: The future of MR will likely include more sophisticated AI algorithms that enhance interactivity and adaptability. For example, AI could personalize the MR experience by tracking user behavior and adapting virtual elements in real-time, creating dynamic environments that respond to each user's actions.

This chapter discussed the **future of VR development**, focusing on the integration of **AI** and the growing influence of **AR** on VR technologies. We explored how **AI** is helping to create more immersive, dynamic VR experiences and how **augmented reality** is shaping the future of **mixed reality**. Real-world examples like **Microsoft HoloLens**, **Magic Leap**, and **Varjo XR-3** show the emerging trends in MR and illustrate how VR and AR are evolving together to create powerful, interactive experiences. As these technologies continue to merge, the potential for immersive and adaptable VR experiences will increase, opening new possibilities for both developers and users alike.

CHAPTER 23

ADVANCED VR PROGRAMMING WITH C++

VR-Specific Programming Challenges: Writing High-Performance C++ Code for VR

Developing VR applications involves a unique set of challenges, especially when it comes to optimizing code to run smoothly in real-time. VR experiences need to maintain high **frame rates** (ideally 90 FPS or higher) to ensure smooth and immersive interactions. Writing **high-performance C++ code** is critical for meeting these demands while managing the complexities of the virtual environment.

1. **Frame Rate and Latency Optimization**:
    o   **High Frame Rates**: VR requires consistent, high frame rates to ensure that users do not experience discomfort or motion sickness. Writing efficient C++ code that ensures smooth frame rendering is key. For example, developers must optimize complex algorithms to process and render high-quality visuals without dropping the frame rate.

221

o **Latency Reduction**: VR applications are sensitive to latency between a user's actions and the resulting visual feedback. To minimize latency, developers often need to optimize the data flow between the hardware (headset, controllers) and the VR application. Using **multithreading** in C++ can help separate heavy computational tasks, such as physics calculations or asset loading, to prevent bottlenecks in the main thread.

2. **Memory Management**:

o **Memory Allocation**: Efficient memory management is crucial in VR development. C++ allows developers to manually control memory allocation and deallocation, which can be optimized to minimize resource consumption. This is particularly important for VR, where running out of memory can lead to poor performance or crashes.

o **Garbage Collection**: While C++ does not have built-in garbage collection like some other languages, it gives developers direct control over memory. Proper **pointer management** and **smart pointers** (e.g., **std::unique_ptr**, **std::shared_ptr**) help prevent memory leaks and optimize performance.

3. **Graphics and Rendering Optimization**:

   o **Efficient Rendering Techniques**: VR applications often use **stereoscopic rendering** to produce images for both eyes, which can strain the GPU. To improve performance, you can use techniques such as **culling, level of detail (LOD)** models, and **optimized shaders** to ensure that only relevant parts of the environment are rendered, reducing the computational load.

   o **Double-Buffered Rendering**: VR requires that the application render frames at a high speed. Double buffering (or even triple buffering) is used to ensure that one frame is being rendered while the previous one is being displayed, reducing input lag and preventing visual tearing.

4. **Physics and Interaction Performance**:

   o **Real-Time Physics**: Complex physics simulations in VR must be optimized for performance. C++ allows for custom physics handling where developers can choose the level of detail needed for the simulation. For example, simplified collision detection algorithms or reduced physics calculations for distant objects can help speed up processing.

   o **Efficient Input Handling**: With VR, continuous input from devices like **motion controllers** and

hand tracking systems must be processed quickly and accurately. Writing C++ code that minimizes input lag and ensures that the user's actions are translated smoothly into the virtual world is key for a natural experience.

Extending Unreal Engine for VR: Customizing Unreal's VR Features with C++

Unreal Engine provides a comprehensive suite of built-in VR features, but there are times when you may need to extend or customize these features to meet the specific needs of your project. Using **C++**, developers can extend the core capabilities of Unreal Engine and create unique VR experiences tailored to the project's requirements.

1. **Creating Custom VR Interaction Systems**:
   o Unreal Engine's **VR Template** provides basic interaction systems like teleportation and object grabbing. However, these may not fit the specific needs of your project, such as custom hand gestures or specific motion controls. With C++, you can extend Unreal's interaction system to create your own custom interaction mechanisms, like adding **advanced object manipulation** or **gesture recognition**.

- **Custom Interaction Model**: For example, if you want to create an interaction where the player can push a button by physically touching a surface, you can use **C++** to define the logic for detecting the player's proximity and interaction gesture.

2. **Customizing Input Handling**:
   - Unreal Engine has built-in input mappings for VR controllers, but sometimes you may need to create custom input systems or handle multiple types of devices (e.g., **Oculus Touch controllers**, **Vive controllers**, **Leap Motion hand tracking**). Using **C++**, you can define **custom input actions** and map specific gestures or button presses to unique actions in your VR experience.
     - For instance, you can customize how the **thumbstick** or **trigger buttons** behave or implement gestures that allow players to swipe, pinch, or hold to trigger specific actions in the virtual world.

3. **Optimizing VR-Specific Cameras**:
   - In VR, the camera system is crucial as it represents the user's view of the virtual world. Unreal's default camera system may need some

tweaks for VR-specific use cases. By extending Unreal's camera system using **C++**, you can implement **head-tracking adjustments, field-of-view customizations**, or **dual-camera setups** (one for each eye).

- You can also program a **dynamic camera system** that adjusts based on the player's movement speed, providing smoother transitions between **teleportation** and **smooth locomotion**, which can help reduce motion sickness.

4. **Performance Tuning and Custom Features**:
   - With C++, you can develop advanced performance optimizations that are specific to VR. Unreal's built-in VR system may not always provide the best performance in all scenarios, so using **C++**, you can directly control how assets are loaded, how the camera system is updated, or how the physics engine interacts with VR objects.
     - For example, you can create a **custom asset loader** that ensures only the assets needed for the current area or scene are loaded into memory, reducing strain on the GPU and improving performance.

5. **Integrating Third-Party SDKs**:

o Sometimes, you may need to integrate third-party VR SDKs (e.g., for **hand tracking, eye tracking**, or **motion controllers**) into your Unreal project. With C++, you can create custom plugins or integrate external libraries into Unreal Engine, providing additional functionality that Unreal's native system does not support.

- For instance, integrating **Leap Motion** for hand tracking requires adding the SDK to Unreal and creating C++ classes to handle input events from the device, allowing you to control the VR experience using gestures.

Real-World Example: A Custom VR Interaction System Developed with C++

Let's explore how a **custom VR interaction system** was developed for a **VR puzzle game**, where players use hand gestures and object manipulation to solve puzzles.

1. **Scenario Setup**:
   o In this VR puzzle game, the player must interact with various objects in the environment, such as rotating levers, stacking blocks, or triggering switches. The game needs a **custom interaction**

system that uses hand gestures to manipulate objects, rather than relying solely on button presses or triggers.

2. **Step 1: Defining Custom Input Methods**:

   o Using **C++**, the development team created a custom input system that maps specific hand gestures to in-game actions. For example, the player could grab an object by making a **pinch gesture**, or rotate a dial by performing a **circular hand movement**. These gestures were recognized using the **Oculus Touch controllers** and **Leap Motion** hand tracking.

3. **Step 2: Custom Interaction Logic**:

   o The developers wrote C++ code that determined how objects could be picked up, moved, and manipulated based on the player's hand movements. For instance, when a player reaches out and pinches their fingers, the game detects the gesture and "grabs" the object, allowing it to be moved through the virtual environment.

     ▪ **Object Interactions**: In the case of rotating levers, the player would use a **circular hand motion**. The C++ code calculates the angle of rotation based on the player's hand movement and applies that change to the lever object in the game world.

4. **Step 3: Performance and Optimization**:

   ○ The team optimized the VR interaction system to ensure smooth performance. They implemented **dynamic asset loading** to minimize lag during object manipulation, and **low-latency tracking** for hand gestures to ensure that interactions felt natural and responsive.

   ○ Additionally, the **collision detection system** was tweaked using C++ to ensure accurate object placement and handling, even in scenarios where objects were being manipulated with subtle gestures.

5. **Step 4: User Testing and Feedback**:

   ○ After implementing the custom interaction system, the team conducted several rounds of user testing. Players tested various gestures and interactions to determine how intuitive and responsive the system was. Based on feedback, the team fine-tuned the gestures, interaction distances, and feedback mechanisms (such as haptic vibration on successful interaction).

6. **Step 5: Final Adjustments and Release**:

   ○ Once the custom interaction system was refined, it was integrated into the full game. The result was a highly immersive VR puzzle game where players could use natural hand gestures to interact with the environment, adding a layer of realism and immersion that was not possible with traditional controller-based systems.

This chapter explored the **advanced use of C++ for VR development**, focusing on the **challenges of writing high-performance code** for VR, the ways in which **Unreal Engine** can be extended for VR projects, and a **real-world example** of a custom VR interaction system developed with C++. By using C++ to create efficient and dynamic VR experiences, developers can push the boundaries of what is possible in immersive environments, making interactions more intuitive, immersive, and performance-optimized. C++ remains an essential tool for creating advanced, high-quality VR experiences in Unreal Engine.

CHAPTER 24

CREATING VR CINEMATICS

Filming VR Cinematics: How to Film and Produce Cinematic Experiences in VR

Creating cinematic experiences in VR is different from traditional filmmaking because the viewer has full control over their perspective. This requires a new approach to filming, directing, and storytelling. In VR, the goal is to immerse the viewer in a scene and give them the sensation of being part of the story, rather than just observing it.

1. **Understanding the Difference between Traditional and VR Cinematics**:
    o **Traditional Filmmaking**: In traditional filmmaking, the director controls the camera angle and movement, guiding the audience's attention to specific aspects of the scene. The viewer is a passive observer, experiencing the narrative through a fixed point of view.
    o **VR Cinematics**: In VR, the viewer is the protagonist, actively participating in the experience by exploring the virtual world. This

requires filmmakers to rethink how they direct a scene, as the viewer can look anywhere, which means the story needs to be told in a more spatial, interactive way.

- **360-Degree Filming**: VR cinematics often use **360-degree video** or immersive environments that allow the viewer to look around freely. Unlike traditional linear filmmaking, VR scenes need to engage the viewer from every angle, creating a fully immersive environment.

2. **Storytelling in VR**:

   o **Immersive Storytelling**: In VR, the story is often told through environmental cues, sound, and character interaction. Filmmakers need to create environments that evoke emotions and immerse the viewer in the narrative, guiding them through the experience using visual and auditory elements.

   o **Non-Linear Storytelling**: Because the viewer can control where they look and explore, VR films often use non-linear storytelling techniques. This can include allowing viewers to uncover different parts of the story as they move through the environment, interact with objects, or follow certain characters.

232

3. **Camera Techniques for VR**:
   o **Fixed vs. Moving Camera**: While traditional filmmaking often involves dynamic camera movements, VR filming must carefully consider the camera's role. In VR, the camera is often stationary (for a more cinematic effect) or follows the action smoothly.
      ▪ **First-Person Perspective**: One common technique in VR cinematics is the **first-person perspective**, where the viewer's viewpoint is that of a character in the story. This creates an incredibly immersive experience, but requires careful attention to avoid disorientation.
      ▪ **Third-Person Perspective**: Some VR films use a third-person perspective, where the viewer may follow a character or remain stationary in a particular position while the character moves through the scene.
4. **Spatial Awareness**:
   o In VR, filmmakers must be aware of **spatial storytelling**—the arrangement of objects and characters in 3D space. This adds a new layer of depth to the narrative, where objects and

characters can surround the viewer, pulling them into the scene.

- o Viewers' **focus** and attention must be carefully managed. For example, sound design, lighting, and motion can be used to guide the viewer's attention toward important elements in the scene, even though they have the freedom to look in any direction.

Tools and Techniques for VR Filmmaking: Using Unreal Engine for Virtual Cinematography

Unreal Engine offers powerful tools for VR cinematography, enabling filmmakers to create highly detailed and interactive VR films. Whether you're capturing 360-degree video or designing fully immersive virtual worlds, Unreal Engine has a range of features to streamline the VR filmmaking process.

1. **Using Unreal Engine's Sequencer for Cinematics**:
   - o **Sequencer** is Unreal Engine's built-in tool for creating cutscenes and animations. It allows filmmakers to control various elements in the scene, including camera movements, lighting, character animations, and more.
   - o **Key Features of Sequencer**:

- **Camera Control**: Set up virtual cameras to capture dynamic movements and smooth transitions. You can create both static and moving shots to simulate traditional cinematic camera movements.

- **Timeline and Keyframes**: Use the timeline in Sequencer to position keyframes for different elements of the scene, such as camera angles, character animations, and lighting changes.

- **Real-Time Rendering**: Unreal Engine allows for real-time rendering, meaning that filmmakers can view the scene and make adjustments on the fly. This is crucial for VR cinematics, as the environment must be fine-tuned to look natural and immersive.

2. **Creating 360-Degree Videos**:

   o Unreal Engine can render **360-degree videos**, which are essential for VR films. With 360-degree cameras or by using special plugins for spherical rendering, filmmakers can create environments that allow the viewer to look in every direction.

   o **Using Cube Map Rendering**: Unreal offers tools to render scenes as **cube maps**, which allow for creating spherical 360-degree content. This involves rendering six faces of a cube, which are then stitched together to create the immersive 360-degree effect.

3. **Lighting for VR Cinematics**:

   o **Dynamic Lighting**: Lighting plays a crucial role in guiding the viewer's focus and enhancing the emotional tone of the scene. Unreal's real-time **dynamic lighting** tools allow filmmakers to manipulate lighting in VR environments, creating realistic shadows, highlights, and atmospheric effects.

   o **Global Illumination**: In VR cinematics, global illumination helps achieve realistic light behavior, allowing light to bounce and interact with surfaces in a natural way. Unreal Engine's **Lumen** system offers high-quality dynamic global illumination that is especially important for immersive environments.

4. **Audio for Immersion**:

   o **Spatial Audio**: To enhance the sense of immersion, spatial audio allows for sound to come from specific directions in the 3D space, creating a more authentic experience. Unreal Engine supports 3D audio, which works alongside the VR visuals to provide a cohesive experience.

- ○ **Dynamic Sound Effects**: Dynamic sound effects, like footsteps or ambient noise, can be integrated into the VR environment to help guide the viewer's experience, much like how sounds are used in traditional films to signal important moments or build tension.

5. **Virtual Camera Systems**:

- ○ **Cinematic Cameras**: Unreal Engine offers highly customizable **virtual camera systems** that can simulate traditional camera movements, such as dolly shots, crane moves, or handheld camera effects. These tools can be used to create traditional cinematography effects within a VR space.

- ○ **Camera Rig**: A custom **camera rig** can be created to simulate physical camera movements, allowing for a more cinematic feel. With VR, you can also explore **camera-free cinematography**, where the user's head movement influences the camera's position and viewpoint.

6. **Interactive Elements in VR Filmmaking**:

- ○ **VR Interaction in Cinematics**: Unlike traditional filmmaking, VR cinematics allow for interaction. This could be as simple as allowing the viewer to choose their perspective at key moments or providing opportunities to explore different aspects of the scene. Unreal Engine's **Blueprints** and **C++** support interactive elements, allowing the audience to influence the narrative or experience.

Real-World Example: Making a VR Short Film Using Unreal Engine

Let's walk through the development of a **VR short film** created using **Unreal Engine**, focusing on the creative process and technical challenges involved in bringing the story to life in VR.

1. **Scenario Setup**:
    o The short film is set in a **futuristic city**, where the viewer plays the role of a detective investigating a mysterious disappearance. The story is told through environmental storytelling, with the viewer exploring different parts of the city to uncover clues.

2. **Step 1: Storyboarding and Scene Planning**:
    o Before using Unreal Engine, the filmmakers create a detailed **storyboard** to outline key scenes, interactions, and narrative beats. Since the viewer has freedom of movement, the story is designed to be explored in a non-linear fashion,

with key events occurring in different locations within the city.

3. **Step 2: Building the Virtual World**:

   o The team uses Unreal Engine to create a detailed **futuristic city environment**. They focus on realistic architecture, lighting, and atmosphere to create an immersive setting. The city is fully navigable, allowing the viewer to explore it from different angles.

   o **360-degree video** is used to create panoramic shots, while dynamic elements like moving vehicles, distant conversations, and interactive objects are added for immersion.

4. **Step 3: Filming with Unreal's Sequencer**:

   o Unreal's **Sequencer** is used to film key cinematic scenes. The virtual camera is programmed to follow specific paths, creating smooth transitions between scenes. For example, the camera might start at street level, then zoom into a building to reveal important clues.

   o **Audio is layered** to match the scene, with ambient city noises and voices coming from specific directions to add depth to the experience.

5. **Step 4: Implementing Interactive Elements**:

   o As the viewer explores the city, they encounter interactive objects such as digital tablets or clues that provide additional information about the investigation. The interaction system is programmed using Unreal's **Blueprints** and **C++** to ensure seamless engagement.

6. **Step 5: Testing and Refining the Experience**:

   o After the film is put together, extensive **user testing** is conducted. Feedback is gathered regarding the ease of interaction, the immersive quality of the visuals and sound, and the overall flow of the narrative.

   o Changes are made to improve the pacing of the story, the effectiveness of the interactive elements, and the comfort of the viewer (e.g., adjusting the movement speed and implementing comfort options like vignette effects to prevent motion sickness).

7. **Step 6: Final Release**:

   o The final VR short film is optimized for multiple VR platforms, including the **Oculus Quest** and **HTC Vive**. The film is packaged for distribution on VR content platforms like **SteamVR** and **Oculus Store**, where it gains attention for its unique narrative style and immersive experience.

This chapter covered the process of creating **VR cinematics**, from filming techniques and storytelling strategies to the technical aspects of using **Unreal Engine** for virtual cinematography. Through **real-time rendering, dynamic lighting**, and **interactive elements**, Unreal Engine allows filmmakers to create highly immersive VR films. The **real-world example** of a **VR short film** demonstrated how these techniques can be applied to create compelling, interactive VR experiences that push the boundaries of traditional filmmaking. As VR technology continues to evolve, the possibilities for cinematic storytelling in virtual environments will only expand.

CHAPTER 25

FUTURE-PROOFING YOUR VR PROJECTS

Staying Up-to-Date with VR Hardware and Software: How to Future-Proof Your VR Projects

As the VR industry continues to grow and evolve, staying ahead of hardware and software trends is crucial to ensure that your projects remain relevant and functional in the long term. New developments in VR headsets, controllers, graphics, and user interfaces can impact the performance, usability, and accessibility of your VR applications. Future-proofing your VR projects means building them in a way that allows them to adapt to these changes without requiring major overhauls.

1. **Understanding Hardware Advancements**:
    o **Next-Gen Headsets**: VR hardware is rapidly advancing, with headsets becoming lighter, more powerful, and more comfortable. Keep an eye on the latest developments in headsets, such as the **Oculus Quest 3**, **Valve Index**, and **PlayStation VR 2**, and their capabilities, such as **improved**

resolution, **better field of view**, and **wireless functionality**.

- o **Tracking and Input Devices**: The next evolution of VR hardware is also likely to include **better hand tracking, eye tracking**, and **haptic feedback** devices. Devices such as **Leap Motion** or **HTC Vive's finger-tracking controllers** are examples of innovations that enhance interaction in VR, offering more precise, natural, and immersive control methods. Anticipating these changes will help you design interaction systems that can easily integrate with upcoming hardware.

- o **Wireless Solutions**: As wireless VR solutions like the **Oculus Quest** become more popular, it's important to develop applications that can run smoothly on both **standalone** and **PC-connected** platforms. This means designing your VR content to work across various configurations, from high-end systems to mobile setups.

2. **Software Development Considerations**:

- o **Cross-Platform Development**: Develop VR projects using software and tools that support **cross-platform compatibility**. Tools like **Unreal Engine** allow you to export content for multiple VR platforms, from **Oculus** and **HTC Vive** to **PlayStation VR** and **Windows Mixed**

Reality. Ensuring your project can be easily adapted to different VR headsets helps future-proof it, as new hardware and platforms emerge.

o **Modular Software Architecture**: Build your software with modularity in mind, using clean coding practices and **modular asset management**. This allows for easier updates, bug fixes, and hardware adaptation in the future without the need for a complete system overhaul.

o **Scalable Content**: VR content should be scalable to fit both low-end and high-end hardware. Use scalable graphics options, **adjustable settings**, and dynamic content generation techniques to ensure that your VR experience runs smoothly on various hardware configurations. Consider the use of **Level of Detail (LOD)** models, **dynamic resolution scaling**, and **adaptive quality settings** to improve performance without sacrificing immersion.

3. **Developing for Emerging Technologies**:

o **5G and Cloud VR**: As **5G networks** become more widespread, cloud-based VR applications will likely gain traction. Consider integrating cloud capabilities into your VR project to support streaming services that reduce the need for powerful local hardware. By future-proofing your

VR applications with **cloud integration**, users can enjoy high-quality VR experiences without requiring advanced hardware.

- o **AI Integration**: As **Artificial Intelligence (AI)** becomes more integrated into VR, it can help personalize experiences, optimize interactions, and automate certain functions (like adjusting difficulty levels or responding to player behavior). Keep an eye on AI advancements that can enhance immersion and interactivity in your VR projects.

Evolving Standards and Practices: Understanding the Trends and Changes in VR Development

VR development is an evolving field, and staying informed about the latest standards and practices is essential for creating sustainable and adaptable VR applications. As VR technology improves and the user base grows, there are several important trends and changes that developers must be aware of to ensure their projects remain on the cutting edge.

1. **New Interaction Paradigms**:
    - o **Natural User Interfaces (NUIs)**: The future of VR interaction will rely on **natural user interfaces**—where users interact with virtual

245

environments using intuitive gestures, voice commands, and eye movements. Technologies such as **eye tracking**, **hand gestures**, and **voice recognition** will continue to advance, enabling more natural and seamless ways to interact with virtual worlds.

o **Mixed Reality (MR)**: The lines between **virtual reality (VR)** and **augmented reality (AR)** are beginning to blur, with **mixed reality (MR)** offering new ways to experience digital content within the real world. As MR technology evolves, developers will need to adapt their VR projects to allow for integration with real-world objects and environments. **MR headsets**, such as the **Microsoft HoloLens** and **Magic Leap**, will continue to influence the development of both VR and AR experiences.

2. **User Comfort and Accessibility**:

o **Reducing Motion Sickness**: One of the main hurdles to wider VR adoption is **motion sickness**. The development of **comfort modes**, such as **teleportation locomotion** and **snap turning**, has helped address this issue, but there are always new techniques being developed to improve comfort. Future VR experiences will likely include more customizable comfort settings, such as adjustable field-of-view (FOV) and dynamic movement options, to cater to different users' preferences and sensitivities.

- ○ **Accessible Design**: As VR becomes more mainstream, ensuring that it is **accessible to everyone** is crucial. This includes making VR experiences available to people with disabilities, such as those who are **blind** or **hard of hearing**. Developers should pay attention to accessibility guidelines and integrate features such as **audio cues**, **subtitles**, **handicap-friendly controllers**, and **adaptive interfaces** to ensure inclusivity.

3. **Networking and Social VR:**

- ○ **Multiplayer VR**: As multiplayer experiences in VR become more common, developers will need to stay on top of trends in **networking** and **multi-user interactions**. VR experiences where players can interact with each other in real-time present challenges in terms of synchronization, latency, and data management. Future VR projects will increasingly incorporate **social features**, such as **avatars**, **voice chat**, and **shared experiences**, creating more **immersive multiplayer worlds**.

- ○ **Virtual Worlds**: As the concept of **the metaverse** continues to gain traction, VR development will need to evolve to support persistent, interconnected virtual worlds. This means developers will need to understand how to create seamless online environments where users can interact with each other and digital assets in shared, persistent spaces. The metaverse will require complex **networking systems**, **cloud storage**, and **cross-platform compatibility**.

4. **Content Delivery and Distribution**:

   o **Subscription Models**: As VR content grows, new ways of delivering and monetizing VR experiences will emerge. Subscription-based models for VR content, similar to **Netflix** or **Spotify**, are becoming more popular, where users can access a library of VR content for a monthly fee.

   o **VR Content Platforms**: As VR platforms become more integrated with other forms of media, developers will need to stay up-to-date with evolving content delivery systems. Platforms like **Oculus Store**, **SteamVR**, and **PlayStation VR** will continue to evolve, and developers must be aware of the distribution requirements, community features, and monetization opportunities each platform offers.

Real-World Example: A Look at How Early VR Projects Adapted to Newer Technologies

Let's take a look at how **early VR projects** adapted to newer technologies and standards, particularly in the transition from **basic VR systems** (like the early Oculus Rift) to more advanced, standalone VR devices (like the Oculus Quest).

1. **Scenario Setup**:
   - In 2016, when the Oculus Rift and HTC Vive were first released, VR development was still in its infancy. These early systems were tethered to PCs, meaning they required high-end hardware to function effectively, and they had relatively limited processing power and tracking capabilities.

2. **Step 1: Transition to Standalone Devices**:
   - With the introduction of the **Oculus Quest** in 2019, VR projects had to adapt to standalone, **wireless systems** with less computing power. Unlike PC-connected VR headsets, the Quest had its own processing unit, meaning developers had to optimize their games and experiences for less powerful hardware. For instance, developers had to reduce asset quality or use simpler shaders to maintain smooth performance on the Quest.

3. **Step 2: Expanding Content and Interactivity**:

o Early VR games relied heavily on basic mechanics such as **teleportation** for movement and **simple hand controllers** for interaction. With advancements in hand tracking and more sophisticated controllers, developers were able to add **more immersive and interactive mechanics** to VR, including **grabbing objects**, **gesture controls**, and **natural locomotion**. These updates helped improve user experience and interaction, especially with the release of the Oculus Quest's **hand tracking** feature in 2019.

4. **Step 3: Adapting to Newer VR Standards**:

o As VR headsets evolved to include more **advanced features** (such as **eye tracking**, **better controllers**, and **improved graphics**), developers adjusted their designs to accommodate these upgrades. For instance, many early VR games were designed for **teleportation-based locomotion**, which was ideal for reducing motion sickness. As the hardware became more powerful and the graphics improved, developers could incorporate **smooth locomotion** and **dynamic environments**, offering a more immersive experience.

5. **Step 4: Supporting Cross-Platform Play**:

o   As the VR landscape grew more fragmented, developers began to prioritize **cross-platform compatibility**, enabling players on different devices (like the Oculus Rift, Quest, or HTC Vive) to interact within the same game world. This adaptability was crucial for keeping players engaged and creating a larger user base for VR games.

This chapter explored strategies for **future-proofing VR projects**, focusing on staying up-to-date with evolving **hardware and software**, understanding changing **industry standards**, and adapting to new technologies. We also looked at how **early VR projects** adapted to emerging technologies, such as the shift from tethered VR systems to standalone devices like the Oculus Quest. By following these best practices, VR developers can ensure that their projects remain relevant, accessible, and high-performing as VR technology continues to evolve.

251

CHAPTER 26

TROUBLESHOOTING COMMON VR DEVELOPMENT ISSUES

Common VR Development Errors: How to Fix Performance Drops, Glitches, and Crashes

When developing VR experiences, various issues can arise that impact performance, stability, and user experience. Performance drops, graphical glitches, and crashes can severely disrupt the immersive quality of VR, leading to a poor user experience. Identifying and fixing these issues early on is crucial for delivering a smooth and enjoyable VR experience.

1. **Performance Drops**:
   - o **Frame Rate Drops**: One of the most common issues in VR development is **frame rate drops**, which can cause nausea and discomfort for users. A consistent frame rate of 90 FPS or higher is essential for a comfortable VR experience. When frame rates drop, users may experience stuttering, lag, or dizziness.
     - ▪ **Solution**: To resolve frame rate issues, optimize both the game's **graphics** and

code. Start by reducing the number of polygons in 3D models, using **Level of Detail (LOD)** models, and simplifying complex shaders. Also, ensure that background processes, such as physics calculations or AI routines, are not overloading the CPU or GPU.

- **Profiling Tools**: Use Unreal Engine's **Profiler** tool to analyze performance and identify bottlenecks in the rendering pipeline, such as inefficient lighting, overdraw, or unoptimized assets.

2. **Glitches and Artifacts**:

   o **Graphical Glitches**: In VR, graphical glitches can break the immersion, causing artifacts like texture pop-ins, lighting inconsistencies, or clipping errors. These glitches are often the result of insufficient optimization or issues with the rendering process.

      - **Solution**: Address these glitches by refining your assets and ensuring textures are properly baked and optimized for VR. Avoid using overly detailed textures in the distance that could slow down rendering. Ensure that your **collision meshes** and **object boundaries** are accurately defined to prevent clipping, where objects pass through each other.

- **Graphics Settings**: In Unreal, use **culling** techniques to avoid rendering objects that are not visible to the player, and adjust **shadow quality** and **reflection settings** to improve overall performance without sacrificing visual quality.

3. **Crashes and Freezes**:
   - **Application Crashes**: Crashes in VR applications can be caused by a variety of issues, including memory leaks, errors in code, or faulty hardware interactions. Crashes can occur unexpectedly, especially during intense or resource-heavy actions within the VR experience.

     - **Solution**: To resolve crashes, start by using **logging tools** and **crash report analyzers** to track down where the error occurs in the code. Make sure to implement **exception handling** in your C++ code to prevent crashes from unhandled errors.

     - **Memory Management**: Monitor memory usage during runtime to identify **memory leaks** and ensure efficient memory management. Use Unreal's **memory profiler** to spot excessive memory allocation or unnecessary data persistence, and ensure objects are properly garbage collected when they are no longer needed.

4. **Input and Tracking Issues**:

   o **Controller Tracking Problems**: Issues with **controller tracking** can lead to input lag, unresponsive controls, or inaccurate motion tracking. These problems are typically caused by poor calibration, interference, or limitations of the hardware itself.

   ▪ **Solution**: Ensure that the tracking system is properly calibrated, and use **sensor fusion techniques** to improve the accuracy of the controller's position in 3D space. If you're working with hand tracking or motion controllers, make sure the controllers have clear line-of-sight to the tracking sensors and that their firmware is up-to-date.

VR Testing and Debugging: Best Practices for VR QA and Bug Testing

Testing and debugging VR projects presents unique challenges compared to traditional game development. VR experiences require **rigorous testing** to ensure that the experience is smooth, immersive, and free of glitches that could ruin the player's experience.

1. **Early and Frequent Testing**:
    o   **Start Early**: Testing should begin as soon as possible in the development process, ideally during the **prototype stage**. Early testing can help identify key issues with user experience, comfort, and performance before they become difficult to address later in development.
    o   **Frequent Iteration**: Since VR experiences can vary greatly between different hardware platforms, it is crucial to test often and on multiple devices. Regularly build and test your VR project on target platforms, such as **Oculus Quest**, **HTC Vive**, or **PlayStation VR**, to ensure compatibility and optimal performance.
2. **Performance and Stress Testing**:
    o   **Frame Rate and Latency Testing**: Use Unreal Engine's **FPS counters** and other profiling tools to monitor the frame rate and latency during

gameplay. VR applications must maintain a consistent 90 FPS or higher, so any drops in frame rate should be addressed immediately.

- o **Stress Testing**: VR applications are often complex, involving intricate models, physics, and lighting effects. Stress testing helps you identify performance bottlenecks and issues that may only appear under heavy loads. This includes testing the game with a high number of assets, objects, and dynamic systems active simultaneously.

3. **User Comfort Testing**:

- o **Motion Sickness and Discomfort**: One of the biggest challenges in VR testing is minimizing **motion sickness**. Test your application with a variety of users who have different sensitivity levels. Implement features like **teleportation** or **snap turning** to reduce discomfort for players who are sensitive to movement.

- o **Usability and Interaction**: Conduct usability testing to ensure that interactions in the VR world feel natural and intuitive. Test how users interact with menus, objects, and in-world physics. Pay attention to areas where users struggle to understand or manipulate virtual objects and make adjustments based on feedback.

4. **Bug Reporting and Debugging Tools**:

- o **Use Unreal's Debugging Tools**: Unreal Engine provides a suite of debugging tools, such as the **Blueprint Debugger**, **Visual Studio**, and the **Log Output** system, to help trace and fix bugs. Utilize these tools to check for issues in your code and analyze performance data.

- o **Crash and Bug Reporting**: Implement crash-reporting and bug-tracking systems to collect feedback on any crashes or glitches users experience during play. Services like **Unreal's Crash Reporter** or third-party tools like **BugSplat** or **HockeyApp** can help you gather detailed reports to resolve issues more efficiently.

5. **User Testing with Feedback Loops**:

- o **User-Centered Testing**: Regularly involve end-users in the testing process to gather feedback on usability, interaction, and immersion. Pay attention to how players react to different experiences, such as handling objects or navigating in the virtual world.

- o **Post-Testing Surveys**: After testing, provide users with surveys to collect more detailed feedback on their experience. Ask them about comfort, control systems, interaction mechanisms, and any issues they encountered during the testing phase.

Real-World Example: Solving a Performance Issue in a Large VR Project

Let's take a look at a real-world example of how performance issues were identified and resolved in a **large VR project** developed using Unreal Engine.

1. **Scenario Setup**:
   - A development team was working on a **VR game** set in a large open-world environment with detailed assets, dynamic weather systems, and complex physics. During testing, the team noticed **frame rate drops** and **stuttering**, especially in high-intensity areas of the game with many objects or NPCs.

2. **Step 1: Identifying the Performance Bottleneck**:
   - The first step was to use Unreal's **Profiler** tool to identify the source of the frame rate drops. The team found that the **dynamic weather system**, particularly the real-time fog and rain effects, was consuming an excessive amount of GPU power. Additionally, there were several high-poly models in the environment that weren't properly optimized for VR.

3. **Step 2: Optimizing Assets**:

- o The development team reduced the polygon count of distant objects using **Level of Detail (LOD)** models and simplified the textures of large environmental assets. They also compressed the fog and rain effects to lower the graphical load without sacrificing visual quality.

4. **Step 3: Implementing Performance Solutions**:

- o **Culling**: The team implemented **culling** techniques to ensure that only the visible parts of the environment were rendered, further improving performance. They also used Unreal's **Occlusion Culling** to ensure that objects not in the player's line of sight were not rendered at all.

- o **Lighting Optimization**: The team adjusted the lighting system, replacing dynamic shadows with **baked shadows** in certain areas to reduce GPU strain.

5. **Step 4: Testing and Refining**:

- o After implementing the optimizations, the team tested the game again on the target VR hardware. The frame rate improved significantly, and the performance issues were resolved. They also tested the game on different VR platforms to ensure it ran smoothly across all devices.

6. **Step 5: Finalizing the Game**:

o With performance issues fixed, the development team continued refining the game's mechanics and user experience. They conducted additional rounds of usability testing to ensure that the VR experience remained comfortable and immersive for all players, especially in complex or high-stress environments.

This chapter focused on **troubleshooting common VR development issues**, such as performance drops, glitches, and crashes. We discussed the importance of **testing and debugging** in VR development, highlighting best practices for performance optimization, bug tracking, and user feedback. The **real-world example** of solving a **performance issue in a large VR project** demonstrated how developers can use Unreal Engine's tools to identify bottlenecks, optimize assets, and improve overall performance, ensuring a smoother and more immersive VR experience.

CHAPTER 27

CONCLUSION AND NEXT STEPS

Recap of Key Concepts: A Quick Review of the Main Lessons in the Book

As we conclude this guide, let's revisit the most important lessons and takeaways from the journey of creating immersive VR experiences with Unreal Engine:

1. **Foundations of VR Development**:
    - o We began by understanding **virtual reality** and how it differs from traditional gaming, exploring key concepts like **immersion**, **interaction**, and **presence**.
    - o Unreal Engine emerged as a powerful tool for VR development, offering both **Blueprints** for visual scripting and **C++** for more advanced, customizable VR programming. We saw how Unreal's flexibility makes it an ideal choice for VR developers.
2. **VR Hardware and Software**:
    - o We covered the importance of **VR hardware**, including headsets, controllers, and sensors, and

how each piece of equipment influences user experience. Understanding hardware is essential to designing VR experiences that are optimized for different platforms.

- We explored how to **build VR projects** using Unreal Engine, setting up a new project and choosing the right VR template, then moving on to create interactive environments with **motion controls** and **locomotion systems**.

3. **Advanced VR Development**:

- Delving deeper, we explored **advanced VR interaction techniques**, creating custom control schemes, and managing **complex physics simulations** in virtual spaces.

- We tackled **performance optimization**, ensuring that VR experiences run smoothly by addressing issues like **frame rate drops**, **latency**, and **input lag**. Additionally, we examined how to implement **spatial audio** to enhance immersion.

4. **Creating Immersive Cinematics and VR Content**:

- We introduced **VR cinematics**—how to film and produce engaging, interactive stories in VR using tools like **Unreal Engine's Sequencer** for camera control, animation, and immersive world-building.

o We discussed **storytelling techniques** in VR, emphasizing non-linear experiences that encourage the player's exploration and engagement.

5. **Testing, Debugging, and Troubleshooting**:

o We highlighted the importance of **testing** throughout the development process, from early builds to final product, including **performance testing, user comfort**, and bug fixing. Testing ensures the best possible user experience and prevents issues like **motion sickness, glitches**, or crashes from undermining your work.

6. **Future-Proofing and Emerging Trends**:

o We also explored the **future of VR** development, emphasizing the importance of keeping up-to-date with the latest VR hardware and software trends. Integrating emerging technologies like **AI, AR**, and **cloud-based VR** will be crucial in staying competitive and ensuring your projects remain relevant.

o We explored how to adapt to **evolving standards** in VR, understanding how **new input methods, mixed reality** environments, and **cross-platform compatibility** are reshaping VR development.

Your Path as a VR Developer: Guidance on Where to Go Next in Your VR Development Journey

Congratulations on completing this guide! But this is just the beginning of your VR development journey. Now that you have a strong foundation, here's how you can continue to grow and advance your skills in the VR space:

1. **Continue Building and Experimenting**:
   - Keep developing your **VR projects**! The best way to hone your skills is by working on real-world applications. Create prototypes, experiment with new interaction systems, and keep testing your ideas. Build small, focused projects that challenge you to explore new areas of VR development.

2. **Contribute to the VR Community**:
   - The **VR development community** is constantly growing and evolving. Participate in **forums**, attend **conferences** (such as **GDC** or **Oculus Connect**), and engage with other developers to learn and share knowledge. Joining **online communities** (like **Reddit's r/virtualreality**, **Unreal Engine forums**, or **Discord servers**) can provide you with valuable feedback and help you grow as a developer.

3. **Learn from Others**:

- o Check out **VR open-source projects**, tutorials, and case studies from successful VR developers. Look for inspiration in how other developers overcome common challenges in VR design, from **creating realistic environments** to **handling complex input systems**.

4. **Focus on Specializing**:
   - o VR is a wide field that covers many different areas, including **game development, simulation, architecture, medical VR**, and **training systems**. As you continue to grow, consider specializing in one area to become an expert. For instance, you could focus on creating **VR simulations for education**, or you could specialize in **high-quality VR cinematics** or **real-time performance optimization**.

5. **Explore VR with Emerging Technologies**:
   - o The integration of **AI, machine learning**, and **cloud-based VR systems** will play an increasing role in future VR development. Look for opportunities to experiment with these technologies, and explore their potential in creating more personalized, dynamic VR experiences.

6. **Publish and Share Your Work**:

- o Once you've created your VR projects, consider publishing them on **VR content platforms** such as **Steam, Oculus Store**, or **PlayStation VR Store**. Share your work on social media, on **YouTube**, or with the wider VR community. Building a **portfolio** and sharing your projects can lead to job opportunities, collaborations, and funding for larger projects.

Real-World Example: Stories from Successful VR Developers

Let's take a look at some inspiring stories from successful VR developers who have made significant impacts on the industry.

1. **John Carmack - Oculus**:
   - o One of the biggest names in the VR industry is **John Carmack**, who was the CTO of Oculus VR. Carmack's work in VR development revolutionized the field by making VR systems more accessible and practical for consumers. His focus on **high-performance rendering** and **optimization** in VR allowed Oculus to deliver high-quality VR experiences.
   - o **Key Takeaway**: Carmack's story teaches us the importance of **optimizing performance** and the **technical aspects** of VR development. He

267

demonstrated that **efficiency in coding** and pushing the limits of hardware can create impactful VR experiences.

2. **Zach Gage – 'SpellTower VR'**:

   o **Zach Gage** is an indie developer who created **SpellTower VR**, a VR puzzle game that merges traditional gameplay with immersive VR environments. Despite being a relatively small developer, Gage utilized Unreal Engine to create a game that stands out for its simplicity and engaging mechanics.

   o **Key Takeaway**: Gage's story highlights the power of **small-scale development**. By focusing on **innovative gameplay** and **user-friendly design**, developers can create successful and popular VR projects without needing massive resources.

3. **Beat Games – Beat Saber**:

   o One of the most successful VR titles to date, **Beat Saber**, was created by **Beat Games**, a small indie team. Beat Saber combined **rhythm-based gameplay** with VR's immersive potential, creating a viral success that attracted millions of players. The team's focus on **user comfort** (via smooth locomotion and motion sickness prevention) and **engaging gameplay mechanics** helped make it a staple of VR gaming.

- o **Key Takeaway**: Beat Games' success shows that **VR game development** can be incredibly rewarding when the experience is **fun**, **comfortable**, and **accessible**. Pay attention to **user experience** and **engagement**—these are the qualities that can drive a game to success.

4. **Viro Media – Immersive Education**:

- o **Viro Media**, a company focused on **VR for education**, has built a platform for creating interactive, educational VR experiences. They've worked on projects that use VR to teach everything from science and history to medicine. Their projects show how **VR can be a powerful tool for immersive learning**.

- o **Key Takeaway**: As VR technology matures, its potential in **education and training** will continue to grow. Developers interested in this area can create **meaningful applications** by focusing on interactivity, immersion, and **real-time feedback** to enhance learning outcomes.

Conclusion:

As you embark on your journey as a **VR developer**, remember that this is an exciting, rapidly evolving field with endless possibilities. By staying up-to-date with the latest hardware and software, experimenting with new technologies, and focusing on user experience, you'll be well on your way to creating successful and immersive VR experiences. Keep learning, testing, and innovating, and don't be afraid to push the boundaries of what VR can achieve. The future of VR development is in your hands— make the most of it!